Adventure and Art
The First One Hundred Years of Printing

An Exhibition of
Books, Woodcuts, and Illustrated Leaves
Printed between 1455 and 1555

November 17, 1998 – April 15, 1999
Rutgers University Libraries Special Collections
and University Archives
Rutgers, The State University of New Jersey

CURATED BY
Barbara A. Shailor
Leonard Hansen
Michael Joseph

EDITED BY
Paul Needham and Michael Joseph

Published by Rutgers University Libraries
Rutgers, The State University of New Jersey
New Brunswick, NJ

Published by Rutgers University Libraries
Rutgers, The State University of New Jersey
New Brunswick, New Jersey

Distributed by Rutgers University Press

ISBN: 0-8135-2727-9

ON52–1999

Table of Contents

Catalog to the Exhibition

Acknowledgments

Producing an exhibition and catalog of this nature requires many talented people collaborating at every stage of a long and complex process. My gratitude extends to all of them. I would particularly like to thank the cocurators of the exhibition, Dr. Barbara Shailor, Dean of Douglass College, whose superlative keynote essay, and whose guidance in material selection, organization, and presentation, deserve our deepest and lasting admiration; and Leonard Hansen, Class of '43, whose generous gift of many rare and unique materials places second in our affection only to the inspiration he provided us through his devotion to the history of the book and his love of libraries. It is our hope that through *Adventure and Art*, the students of Rutgers, The State University of New Jersey, will find the selfsame spirit of discovery and wonder.

We also are deeply indebted to Paul Needham, Librarian of the Scheide Library, Princeton University Library, for casting a meticulous eye over our earliest materials and identifying items of historical significance, and for building citations for the incunabula included in the first section of our catalog; and to Dr. Remiggio Pane, Emeritus Professor of Italian Studies, for his characteristically gracious, whimsical, and learned assistance in shaping the Italian section of our exhibition catalog; to Harry W. Blair, and Drs. Consuelo and Dennis Dutschke, for their scholarly responses to our persistent inquiries on early Italian humanism; to Michael Joseph, our library liaison, for coordinating the efforts of the curators and for drafting the exhibition catalog in conjunction with Paul Needham; to Halina R. Rusak, Art Librarian, for pointing out the loveliest pieces in our collection for our "Illustration and Early Printing" section; and, certainly not least of all, to my exhibition team—Judith K. Brodsky, Director, Center for Innovative Print and Paper; John Ross, Chairman of the Board of the Center for Book Arts; Dr. Robert Sewell, Associate University Librarian for Collection Development; and Ronald L. Becker, Head, Special Collections and University Archives. Their exemplary commitment to learning, to the traditional role of the library, and to the goals and objectives of Rutgers, The State University of New Jersey, helped to set us on a course that could not fail.

I would also like to thank various people in the Libraries who contributed time and expertise: Janet Riemer, Conservation Archivist, and Maria Pisano, for preparing many of the exhibits for display; Ruth Simmons, Exhibitions Coordinator; and Carmen Godwin, for exquisitely designing the individual exhibition cases; Albert C. King, Manuscripts Librarian, for his advice on the selection of maps; and Sara Harrington, a doctoral student in the Art History Department, for her scholarly preparation of "Illustration and Early Printing." Alan Goldsmith, university photographer, deserves special acknowledgment for his superb photography, as does Christine Becker for proofreading, and Rutgers' Office of University

Publications for the loving preparation of the manuscript.

Several individuals and institutions have provided loans of material and financial assistance for this exhibition. I especially thank Dr. Martin Picker, Emeritus Professor of Music; Dr. Hans Fischer, Professor of Nutritional Biochemistry; the Princeton University Library; the Class of '43; and the Special Collections and University Archives Gift Fund.

Every exhibition in the Rutgers University Libraries affords us fresh opportunity to acknowledge our gratitude to the Friends of the Library for their dedicated support of our efforts to make the Rutgers University Libraries a central place in the intellectual life of our campus, and of the state of New Jersey.

Marianne Gaunt
University Librarian

Rutgers Special Collections and Its Rare Books

by Robert G. Sewell

Associate University Librarian for Collection Development and Management,
Special Collections and University Archives, Rutgers, The State University of New Jersey

*A*dventure and Art: The First One Hundred Years of Printing commemorates the six hundredth anniversary of the birth of Johann Gutenberg, the inventor of printing from movable type. It is the realization of a long-held dream of mine, of Special Collections and University Archives, and of many Friends of the Rutgers University Libraries. One Friend in particular, Leonard Hansen (RC '43), has been an ardent and persistent advocate for book collecting and for the importance of the history of the book in liberal arts education, as his reminiscence in this catalog eloquently attests. In addition to allowing the Libraries to borrow several beautiful incunabula and rare illustrated leaves for the purpose of this exhibition, Mr. Hansen has served as one of the exhibition's curators. We also are very privileged to have had as our other cocurator, Dr. Barbara Shailor, Dean of Douglass College and Professor of Classics. In addition to undertaking the curatorial tasks of material selection and organization, Dr. Shailor has written the catalog's keynote essay on the special relevance of Gutenberg's invention, and the transition from manuscript-based learning to print, to the information issues leading us into the twenty-first century.

Dean Shailor is no stranger to catalogs of rare materials from the medieval and Renaissance periods. She produced a wonderful three-volume catalog, *Catalogue of Medieval and Renaissance Manuscripts in the Beinecke Rare Book and Manuscript Library, Yale University* published by Medieval & Renaissance Texts & Studies, 1984–1992. Building on that work she wrote *The Medieval Book: Illustrated from the Beinecke Rare Book and Manuscript Library,* published by the University of Toronto Press in association with the Medieval Academy of America, now in its third edition.

In addition to the inherent interest of the materials and the way they are presented here, what excites me about this exhibition and catalog is the light they shed on a lesser known component of Special Collections and University Archives.

Special Collections is rightly known for its comprehensive collections of New Jerseyana, esteemed as one of the finest collections of state and regional history in the country. With holdings from colonial times to the present in all formats (printed books and pamphlets, broadsides, maps, diaries, official and private papers of individuals and organizations, examples of books arts in New Jersey, and realia), the New Jersey collections are unsurpassed in documenting the state's history and culture. Another treasure of Special Collections is the internationally known William Elliot Griffis Collection. Also well represented are collections relating to the consumer movement in the United States and to twentieth-century Latin American society, politics, and culture. The University Archives contains material related to the history of Rutgers that complement Special Collections New Jerseyana in that Rutgers was founded in the colonial period and has had a major impact on the state.

Less known are Special Collections holdings outside of these areas. While not extensive, our rare book holdings include significant and valuable strengths. For instance, our eighteenth-century England collection is characterized by comprehensive collections of Daniel Defoe (1660–1731) and William Cobbett (1763–1835). The first century of printing is an area of the collection that has never before been fully explored. In the course of preparing this exhibition, we identified approximately 175 books printed before 1555, twenty-eight of which are incunabula–books printed before 1501. This especially valued category of early printed books has now been recorded in the Incunable Short Title Catalog (ISTC). According to the ISTC, Rutgers holds three titles for which there are only three other known copies in the United States, two for which there is only one other copy in the United States, and an astounding five which are unique in the United States. Among those titles for which Rutgers has the only copy in the country, Cato's *Disticha de moribus...* (Antwerp, 1487) is one of four known copies in the world, and Cicero's *Epistolae selectae* (Rome, about 1485) and Stephanus Fliscus, *Sententiarum variationes, seu Synonyma...* (Paris, about 1492) exist in only one other copy.

Rutgers is indeed proud to own such rare incunables. But as S.H. Steinberg asserts in *Five Hundred Years of Printing,* the strict cut off date of 31 December 1500 for incunabula forms, from the perspective of scholarship, an arbitrary distinction. "This date cuts right across the most fertile period of the new art, halving the lives of some of its greatest practitioners, such as Anton Koberger, Aldus Manutius, Anthoine Verard, and Geoffroy Tory." Rutgers' 150 other titles published between 1501 and 1555 are, as *Adventure and Art* convincingly demonstrates, equally significant and beautiful exemplars of printing during this initial period of creativity and growth.

Adventure and Art

by Barbara A. Shailor

Dean of Douglass College and Professor of Classics
Rutgers, The State University of New Jersey

An event of extraordinary historical significance occurred in Germany in the middle of the fifteenth century. At his workshop in Mainz, Johann Gutenberg invented the concept of printing from movable metallic type. Using this state-of-the-art technology, Gutenberg was the first to mass produce approximately 180 copies of a large, magnificent two-volume Bible today known as the "Gutenberg Bible."

What happened in the next hundred or so years of printing after this remarkable *editio princeps* of the Bible is the story of this exhibition and catalog. It is not, however, a taxonomy of type fonts through the decades, but a brief synopsis of the "adventure and art" (*Afentur und Kunst*) of early printing, as Gutenberg himself described his initial experiments. The first printed books are artifacts that tell us about the survival and transmission of texts, in Latin and the national languages; about the cultures that produced and read the books; and about the incredible dissemination of knowledge that happened at the end of the Middle Ages and the beginning of the Renaissance. In addition, a discussion of the first hundred years of printing encourages us to think critically about the future of printing and publishing in the present digital age.

The invention of printing can perhaps find an analogy in the Roman god Janus—a double-faced deity who could look back toward the past and at the same time forward toward the future. Gutenberg and his colleagues drew upon the models of books that were developed during the previous millennium. The initial printed volumes replicated, often meticulously, the hand-produced manuscript books, which were copied by scribes and decorated in gold and colors by artists.

The very shape of the printed book, including the one you now hold in your hands, had been determined by the fourth century with the emergence and triumph of the parchment codex (or book, as we term it today) over antiquity's roll format: almost always rectangular with the long axis running vertically, the book can be said to derive "naturally" from the rectangular shape of an animal skin. But most early printing, and virtually all of today's, uses paper as its medium, a substance that could be produced in almost any shape or design; and yet, with the early printers as with today's industry, the idea of the rectangular (or sometimes square format for children's books) has remained remarkably constant.

At the same time that the cradle of printing was indebted to the past, Gutenberg and his contemporaries initiated a cultural and intellectual revolution through their texts "written in metal." The invention of printing engendered a subtle but significant shift in the reader's attitude toward the book. The most immediate impact was prompted by sheer numbers: a single scribe, normally speaking, worked from one exemplar and produced one copy; a single printer, with his workshop, produced from 200 to 1,000 printed copies of a text from his single exemplar.

Clearly, the effect on the reading public was to increase suddenly and vastly the possibility of access to the written word. What had been a wealthy person's treasure became over the course of the hundred years covered by this exhibit a normal, everyday object in middle class homes. So valuable were manuscript books in the Middle Ages that they served as collateral in pawn shops, they were bequeathed singly to named individuals, they were inventoried at the death of a prince as part of his worldly wealth.

Within a century after Gutenberg's invention, the only quasi-legal listing of specific copies of books was to be found in library catalogs, where the ultimate purpose was not to appraise wealth, but to provide a means of intellectual retrieval and access. Other lists, such as the *Index librorum prohibitorum* (first issued in 1557), all the way up to modern library catalogs, cite authors and titles, not the actual physical object of the book.

This leads to a second factor in the impact of the printed book: the uniformity internal to a given press run. Gutenberg and his contemporaries were themselves not unaware of this change; a monk in Subiaco, apparently the home of the first printing press in Italy, proposed that his monastery should embrace the new technology, that they should embark upon a program of printing church service books, with the precise and stated intention of encouraging uniform liturgical practice in all monastic houses.

Uniformity in books has become such a standard feature that, for the most part, we no longer recognize the aid it brings to scholarship. If I were not confident that my colleagues in classics were reading the same scholarly edition of Seneca's *Epistles* as I, how could I cite a page reference upon which to comment, to consider, to interpret a particular point in this Latin author's works? Today we cite relatively few texts according to their internal organization; one of the few is the Bible, where we still follow the thirteenth-century citation format of book and chapter; the biblical verse numbering only began with sixteenth-century printed editions.

The rapid availability of books and the uniformity of their texts meant that more people could read books, that more people could converse with one another about their contents; printing contributed to the open access to knowledge and the more broadly based discussion of ideas, whether philosophical, literary, theological, or historical.

The Beginning of Printing

The oldest printed book belonging to the Rutgers University Libraries was published in Cologne about 1467 by the prolific printer, Ulrich Zel (Entry 2, Figure 1). The volume illustrates salient features of early printed books—features that locate printed books in the medieval tradition of handwritten codices.

Modest in appearance, the volume does not have a title page, as most books would today. Rather, it has a simple heading on the first page, with the pertinent information about the author and title of the work in six lines of a slightly larger type font. A statement with similar information appears at the conclusion of the treatise. Neither the name of the printer nor the place and date of printing are provided anywhere in the publication.

The book, which contains a treatise by Johannes Gerson on the ten commandments, confession, and death, is functional rather than elegant and follows the conventions of similar texts in manuscripts. The type font was designed after handwritten models of the day that had numerous abbreviations and letters joined together in ligatures; the font looks remarkably like the script the reader would have discovered in a manuscript version of the same text. Plain initials and paragraph marks, added by hand by a decorator after the pages were printed, alternate in blue and red in order to demarcate important breaks in the text, whereas the initials letters for each sentence were simply stroked in red.

The audience for this volume included students and teachers of theology who were not necessarily interested in the humanistic learning and education being strongly embraced in Renaissance Italy. And printers in fifteenth- and sixteenth-century Cologne specialized in the production of Latin theological texts in the medieval tradition.

As these next two figures demonstrate, at first glance, it may be difficult to distinguish between an early printed book and a hand-produced manuscript, so closely did they follow similar conventions of script, decoration, design, and layout.

Entry 28, Figures 14 and 15 reproduces a splendid leaf from a liturgical manuscript hand produced in Beauvais in Northern France toward the end of the thirteenth century. It is an exceptionally fine Latin Missal written and illuminated with gold and colored completely by hand.

Entry 27, Figure 13 illustrates the opening leaf of a Venetian printing dated 1481 of the ancient historian, Josephus. The text was typeset in metal, but the dense and elaborate border that extends through the upper, inner, and lower margins was delicately added by a professional artist.

There are also other differences. The Beauvais Missal was executed on parchment—animal skin—which for centuries was the preferred material for medieval and Renaissance manuscripts. Although parchment was strong, durable, and capable of great luster when expertly prepared, it was very expensive. A single copy of the Bible, for example, might require the skins of an entire herd of animals. Although already in production in parts of Europe and Asia, with the beginning of printing, paper quickly replaced parchment for book production, and, in fact, all of the early printed books in the Rutgers collection employ paper as the support for the written text. The widespread use of paper and new recipes for ink in the second half of the fifteenth century made possible, at a reasonable cost, the extensive print runs and successive editions of popular works.

What is of greater significance is the respective markets for the two items. The Beauvais Missal would have been made for a wealthy patron who commissioned the volume according to his or her personal aesthetic tastes and financial resources, for every leaf of this manuscript would have been beautifully illuminated. It was too expensive a volume to be produced upon speculation, with the expectation that some person or some institution would acquire it. From the beginning, printing was a commercial venture. Books were printed without specific monasteries or individual collectors as clients for the edition of a given text. The printer had to calculate carefully which authors would sell, how many books to print, who among his present clientele might buy the copies, and how to reach a broader market.

In the case of this Josephus volume, the original artist deliberately left unfilled the circular space in the lower margin. It was anticipated that the person who purchased the book would personalize the copy by adding the family coat-of-arms. Here the arms (still to be identified) have been inserted in ink by a later, unskilled hand.

The origins of the modern printed book are apparent in the splendid Rutgers copy of Suetonius, *Lives of the Twelve Caesars*, produced in Venice by Nicolas Jensen in 1471 (Entry 16, Figure 11). With the revival of classical learning in the Italian Renaissance, printers in Italy mimicked their scribal colleagues, who had been seeking to recapture the simple nature of the scripts used in the tenth and eleventh centuries; they consciously rejected the often difficult to read, angular gothic letters of the later Middle Ages. Jensen created "Roman" types characterized by plain, yet elegant, letters. Even the large, hand-painted faceted initials that introduce each of the twelve *Lives* (e.g., "G" for Germanicus) were modeled after the capitals found carved on ancient monuments from the Roman period. The initials in this volume were faintly outlined first in lead (an early form of pencil), and then colored by an artist of considerable skill.

The Roman typefaces of Nicolas Jensen were to have direct impact on printers for centuries to come. In the late nineteenth century, William Morris, enamored of Jensen's lovely fonts, used them as the basis for his own fine printing.

Transformations

Transformations in the design and execution of the book, some subtle and others more dramatic, occurred in the early decades of printing. In addition, beginning in the 1480s the production of manuscript books began to decline sharply, and the production of printed books increased and dominated the market. As literacy rates and the demand for printed books rose, there was a gradual loss of the individuality with respect to both their text and physical appearance. The almost infinite variety of the hand-produced medieval manuscript gave way to a level of standardization typical in an average print run.

Typology of the Printed Book

The combination of increased demand for the product and the technology of printing required simplification of the process. Printers soon developed formal programs of decoration—initials, borders, and illustrations—that could be integrated into an overall typographical layout for a given volume. Colors and highlighting might be added later by an artist, but the design of the page, including text and illustrations, was predetermined when it was printed.

At the most basic level, woodcuts were substituted for initials. Two volumes illustrate different approaches to standardized alphabets, which eventually replaced initials executed by hand. Both Günther Zainer of Augsburg and Johann Zainer of Ulm were innovators in book illustration and were among the first to use woodcut letterforms in their workshops.

In the *Pantheologica* produced in Augsburg in 1474 by Günther Zainer (who was also a scribe and illuminator by profession), the boldly framed initials, adapted from Gothic manuscript models, were woodcuts later touched with red (Entry 8, Figure 3). In the imposing Bible printed by Johann Zainer in 1480, the lively unframed initials, also woodcuts, are characterized by luscious, intertwining leaves lightly highlighted with red ink (Entry 9, Figure 4).

Extensive sets of woodcut drawings also were created to illustrate books, and the same cuts often were used by different printers for more than one text. In France, illustrated printed books followed the extraordinarily creative tradition of manuscript illumination, whether in books composed in Latin or in French. The edition of the *Legenda aurea sanctorum*, printed in Lyons in 1487 by Martin Huss, offers many fine examples of early woodcut illustration. For each saint discussed by the author, Jacobus de Voragine, a woodcut provides a visual image to underscore the main point of the narrative. In several instances in this volume, the *same* woodcut was used multiple times to represent different saints; for example, there are generic scenes for beheading a martyr, and for a saint either reading a book, presumably the Bible, or merely standing at ease. The illustration of St. Michael killing the dragon reproduced here is plain in its style of execution, yet is vivid in the action depicted (Entry 31, Figure 17). The drawing is unsophisticated by modern standards, but dynamically represents the demise of the monster and the spiritual heroism of St. Michael.

By the time that the edition of Vergil was published in Lyon in 1517, the artistry of book illustration was well established.

Entry 43, Figure 23 reproduces a scene from Book I of Vergil's *Aeneid*. Neptune, Juno, and the winds are depicted in the upper part of the picture, while the ships of Aeneas are buffeted about on the sea below. The text proper of the Latin epic appears in a larger size type font, whereas the series of scholarly commentaries by Servius, Donatus, and other authors surround the text in a smaller size font. The illustration, however, quickly attracts the attention of the reader, not only because of its boldness and detail, but also because of its perfection as an artform.

The physical book as we know it today, complete with title page and pagination, triumphantly emerged from the medieval manuscript conventions. Printers became comfortable with the contrast of black and white, and were increasingly less dependent on the colorful details added by decorators after the text was printed. Workshops also experimented with new concepts for the book, as is evident in a charming world chronicle (*Cronica cronicarum*) published in Paris by François Regnault in 1532 (Entry 33, Figure 18), where a genealogical "tree" is displayed horizontally.

During the fourteenth and fifteenth centuries, large genealogical scrolls, often twenty to thirty feet in length, were copied and illuminated as luxury goods. The scroll was the perfect format for representing the lineage of and relationships among the legendary and historical figures; each strand of history would start at the top of the roll and descend to the bottom. The text, and accompanying illustrations of people and places, descended together vertically.

In the chronicle printed by Regnault, the historical scroll has been transformed into the book format. The genealogical tree is represented by a combination of straight connecting lines and leafy branches that extend horizontally from one opening to the next. The format of this genre of world chronicle was cleverly adapted from a scroll to accommodate the new technology of the printed book.

Vernacular Books

The introduction of printing made it possible to mass produce texts for many different communities of readers. Books containing vernacular literature, vernacular translations of Latin and Greek authors, and multilingual texts were printed in record numbers. Students, scholars, theologians, aristocrats, merchants, and educated men and women were all eager for reading material in their national languages, as well as in Latin, the traditional language of the Church and the law.

In Italy, when publishers began to assess the market for books, Dante, Petrarch, and Boccaccio were among the first authors whose Italian works were printed. The Rutgers copy of the *Divine Comedy* of Dante, produced in Venice in 1497, is a deluxe edition with detailed woodcuts. Anecdotes from the period, in addition to the large number of manuscripts and printed books still extant, demonstrate that everyone in Italy was interested in Dante. Boccaccio lectured about Dante to public audiences in Florence. Members of the middle class were hungrily acquiring books containing Dante's poetry. And even those who could not read were memorizing and reciting his poetry: the short story writer Franco Sacchetti (*novella* 114) tells how Dante was walking down the street in Florence past a blacksmith's shop when he heard his *Divine Comedy* being sung most wretchedly by an artisan in the shop! The Rutgers copy of Dante, with its series of illustrations, was intended for the upper-end of the book-buying market; it was designed for educational purposes, most likely for individuals who were literate, but did not know Latin. The Italian text of Dante, in a somewhat larger type font, is surrounded by the detailed commentary of Cristoforo Landino, also in Italian. Key words and phrases in the margins direct the reader's attention to important points in the commentary, such as references to Plato or Vergil. Each canto has a woodcut that is instructive and intended to help the reader better comprehend the text. For example, Dante is identified by the letter "D" and Vergil by "V" (Entry 18, Figure 5). The illustrations are a didactic, as well as an aesthetic, device for the nonscholarly audience.

In addition to texts originally composed in the national languages, there was an equally strong audience for vernacular translations of classical authors. Since many people did not know enough Latin to read the elegant language of such ancient authors as Caesar, Cicero, or Pliny, many Latin and Greek authors were translated into vernacular languages.

The crisp copy of Josephus preserved at Rutgers that was printed in Strassburg in 1535 illustrates this point (Entry 5, Figure 2). It is a fine example of a classical author whose original work was composed in Greek, then translated into Latin (see also Entry 27), and here into German. Josephus's writings on Jewish history were extremely popular texts throughout the Middle Ages and Renaissance, so it is not surprising that they were translated, copied, and printed many times.

This volume also demonstrates how, just as different scripts were associated with different texts in medieval manuscripts, different type fonts were developed and used for the printed version of different books. Whether published in English, French, or German, a distinctive type font distinguished the vernacular texts from the Latin. In Germany many varieties of this handsome style of type font and decorative initials began to evolve in the fifteenth century and have persisted into the twentieth century, so strongly have they become identified with the language, literature, and culture of the country.

Greek Language and Literature
After the Turks captured Constantinople in 1453, many Greek scholars fled to Italy. They brought with them their knowledge of Greek literature and hundreds of manuscript texts by classical and medieval Greek authors. The intellectual zeal of the Italian humanists for Greek literature created both a strong market for printed books and typographical challenges for the printers.

In the earliest years of printing, whenever Greek words or phrases appeared in a Latin text, the compositor left a space and a scribe entered the Greek text by hand. Throughout the Rutgers copy of the Suetonius text printed by Jenson in 1471, Greek quotations were carefully inserted by a scribe in pale red ink. Soon, however, Greek type fonts, with seemingly innumerable complexities of abbreviations and ligatures, were designed by printers, and Greek authors could be published in their entirety.

The *editio princeps* of Homer, edited by the Greek scholar Demetrius Chalcondyles, was printed in 1488 in Florence by Bartolomeo Libri. This elegant publication, here bound as two volumes, presented the complete corpus of Homer's works, as it was defined in the Renaissance: the *Iliad*, the *Odyssey*, the Homeric

Hymns, and the mock-epic poem the *Battle of the Frogs and the Mice*. This edition, the first major classical Greek author to be typeset, established high standards of scholarship and printing for all subsequent publications in Greek.

Aldus Manutius set up his press in Venice in 1495, where he promoted and revolutionized the publication of Greek texts. More importantly, at the time that Byzantium was disintegrating, Aldus and his press assumed responsibility for preserving the heritage of Greek literature. Aldus created a market niche by concentrating on the texts of previously unpublished Greek authors (e.g., Aristotle and Sophocles), by printing them in small, affordable formats, and by selling them in large numbers throughout Europe. Unlike earlier printers, who produced approximately 200 to 250 copies as an average print run, Aldus usually ran 1,000 copies.

The talents of Aldus can be seen in the typographical challenges of printing a bilingual text, the Greek grammar book of Fra Urbanus Bellunensis published in January of 1497 (Entry 48, Figure 26). In the second half of the fifteenth century there was sufficient interest in Greek language and literature to publish grammars for students. Aldus requested that Urbanus, a teacher in Venice, compose this grammar; the book was so popular that it was reprinted more than twenty times in the sixteenth century.

The Latin and Greek portions of the text are in perfect spatial harmony throughout the volume, with each type font complementing the other. One can understand, based on this bilingual text, how it soon became possible in the early sixteenth century to print the complex polyglot Bible in which the Vulgate Latin, the Greek Septuagint, the original

Hebrew, and the Aramaic exegetical paraphrases are all printed on the same page.

The Readers and Collectors of Early Printed Books

During the Middle Ages the handwritten manuscript book was acquired by monasteries, cathedrals, and other ecclesiastical institutions, for general use rather than for the use of an individual. It was only in the later Middle Ages that "bestsellers," such as the devotional *Book of Hours*, were produced in quantity for the men and women who could afford them.

Many early printed books were also produced for communal use in the medieval tradition. The handsome Latin Bible, published in Lyons in 1512 by Jacques Sacon, is strongly representative of this continuing trend. It is a lectern-style Bible intended for reading and easy reference (Entry 44, Figure 24). Attractively bound in blind-stamped vellum, the volume contains the early inscription of the Benedictine monastery of Ochsenhausen in Württemberg. Whether this monastery was the original owner of the Bible or was the recipient of a donation by a member of the monastic order residing at Ochsenhausen is not known; the Bible was, however, in the monastery's library in the seventeenth century by the time the ownership inscription was recorded: "Monasterij Ochsenhausanj 1631."

Large format religious, patristic, and liturgical books continued to be in demand, but Aldus Manutius first created the fashion in Italy for small, pocket-size books suitable for individual study or meditation. The mass production of compact books for private ownership became a hallmark of the early sixteenth century,

and included thousands of copies of *Books of Hours* that eventually replaced manuscripts (Entry 34, Figure 19).

The introduction of the italic typeface for printing can also be attributed to Aldus—an innovation that facilitated the trend toward a small format for printed books. In the fifteenth century, Italian Renaissance scholars preferred to acquire and to read manuscripts copied either in the round humanistic bookhand that became the model for "Roman" fonts or in the cursive script popular in the second half of the century. It was this humanistic cursive script, influenced by the elegant and elongated letterforms of the papal chancellery, that served as the exemplar for the commercial italic type fonts of the Aldine press. The narrow, gently sloping script allowed more text to be printed on a single page and contributed to the development of the Aldine "pocketbook."

Although Aldus may be the individual who introduced italic type to printing, the elegance of this style of type can perhaps best be appreciated in the work of somewhat later printers of the sixteenth century. For example, the exceptionally fine calligraphic italic designed by Ludovico degli Arrighi drew heavily upon his skills as a writing-master in Rome (Entry 51, Figure 28). Arrighi's italic, with its attenuated ascenders on letters such as *l*, *h*, and *b*, and long curving descenders on *f* and *p* define a standard of excellence for italic type fonts that still inspires admiration in a modern reader. On a more functional level, the scholar-printers Robert and Henri Estienne both used a less self-conscious design of italic type font in their Parisian workshop (Entry 50, Figure 27). Publications, such as their handbooks of classical authors (including the lovely Rutgers copy of the agricultural treatises of Cato and Varro), demonstrate the pervasiveness of italic font throughout Europe.

The concept of printing books that were both inexpensive and portable spread rapidly from Italy to other countries, because of the expanding market of middle-class readers such as doctors, lawyers, and merchants. Even fake "Aldines" began to appear, as commercial printers recognized the potential for explicating the new trend. The Rutgers collection has at least four volumes, influenced by the Aldine innovation that "smaller is better." Two deserve special notice.

The first, printed in Paris in 1541 by Pierre Regnault, contains selections from the Latin Vulgate version of the Bible, and not the complete text. It does have a lovely series of illustrations, including the proverbial Job on the Dunghill (Entry 37, Figure 20). We can easily imagine the owner of this little book contemplating both the words and pictures in private study or meditation.

The second volume prints the French verses of the court poet, Jean Marot. It is a fine example of a vernacular pocketbook that also includes a number of French translations of classical authors such as Vergil and Ovid. Knowledge of the original Latin text was not required by the reader of this book. In Entry 39, Figure 21 we see how the artist has captured the tranquil pastoral setting of Vergil's first *Eclogue*.

Publishers across Europe discovered, as well, that elaborately illustrated volumes on practical or nonreligious subjects were highly marketable. Many of these volumes resemble the "coffee table books" published by specialty presses today.

Two volumes in the Rutgers collection are examples of this genre of book. Printed in Strasburg in 1530–32, the illustrated herbal of Otto Brunfels is a masterpiece of vernacular printing in German. The woodcuts of plants, delicately hand colored, have been spaciously and aesthetically arranged throughout (Entry 12, Figure 9).

The Latin scientific text of Pedianus Dioscorides, published in Frankfurt in 1549, also has extraordinary illustrations, including the multicolored sea serpent in Entry 13, Figure 10. An extensive index of plant names in Greek, Latin, French, and German constitutes a multilingual reference tool for readers from countries across Europe.

Printing promoted a democratization of learning and the spread of knowledge that have continued to the present day. The improvement in literacy, the increase in the number of vernacular texts, and the fact that "good cheap" books became readily available (as the early English printer William Caxton was quick to note) provided the synergistic environment for buying and collecting books. This trend was most remarkable in the Italian Renaissance of the fifteenth century when extensive libraries were amassed by individuals and communities.

Renovated by Cosimo de' Medici in 1440, the Dominican convent of San Marco in Florence became, under his guidance and auspices, the first public library in Italy. Cosimo purchased some collections of books and commissioned other manuscript volumes from the local stationers. Many books entered the library as the result of legacies and gifts.

Among the late fifteenth-century literary figures who became one of the more generous and learned benefactors to the library was the teacher-scholar Giorgio Antonio Vespucci (ca. 1434–1514), the uncle of the navigator Amerigo Vespucci. When Giorgio Antonio entered the convent, he presented at least fifty manuscripts and printed books, with many of them bearing his *ex libris*.

The Rutgers University Libraries preserves in its Special Collections one of the printed books given by Giorgio Antonio to San Marco in 1499, a copy of the letters of the noted humanist Francesco Filelfo, printed in Venice in 1473. The volume contains both Giorgio Antonio's signature (lower margin of the final page: "Liber Georgij Antonij Vespucij"), a notation on the front flyleaf giving the precise location of the book in the library (an early shelf-mark dated 1499: "In Bancho. xxviij [ex parte] occidentis"), and Giorgio Antonio's autograph reference notes in the margins of the text, written for the most part in pale red ink (Entry 19, Figures 6–7).

How appropriate it is that this volume should now find a place at Rutgers University—The State University of New Jersey—and one of the great public universities in the United States. What a splendid home Rutgers is for an early printed book with its own "public" library tradition!

This exhibition and catalog on the first hundred years of printing reaffirm Gutenberg's excitement about the "adventure and art" of printed books. The books themselves help us appreciate the revolution that Gutenberg and his colleagues initiated and how it contributed to the Renaissance of thought at the end of the fifteenth and beginning of the sixteenth centuries.

The early printers envisioned a world where many people, rather than a restricted few, could acquire and read texts. Their vision and the development of the mass-produced book were contemporary with and contributed to sea changes in the sixteenth century, not the least of which was the Reformation. The availability of the printed word encouraged widespread and profound theological discourse, including the provocative reevaluation of the past by Erasmus and Luther. Clearly, Gutenberg, Jensen, Manutius, and colleagues had a limited understanding of the impact they would have on the future of the world. They could never have imagined the directions in which printing would influence civilization and how they, working in their small communities of the fifteenth century, would shape the way we have viewed and transmitted knowledge for centuries.

Today—more than 500 years after the invention of printing—the role of the printed book in our society is being reassessed because of the introduction of electronic databases, the exponential proliferation of information technology, and the development of virtual publishing. The potential for reaching new audiences in a global community through electronic means is extraordinary, yet the full extent of that potential remains uncertain.

Set in the context of the digital age, the critical study of early printing is perhaps more fascinating than it has been in previous decades or centuries. We appreciate in new ways the physical nature of the book that we hold in our hands. Its value as an artifact and historical document from the distant past is affirmed. We understand, as well, that early printed books do not just convey the words of an author, but embody and symbolize the cultures from which they arose: any given book's message is conveyed through the use of a particular type font, its layout, the interplay among text, commentary and illustration from one page opening to the next, its binding, and also through the annotations of the generations of readers who owned or used a book. Each extant volume has its own history, from the day it was produced in a commercial printshop in Mainz, Venice, or Lyons, to the present.

The digital revolution promises to bring further "adventure and art" to all of us who are intellectually excited by reading, writing, learning, and books. Just as early printers were concerned with establishing the definitive text of Homer or Vergil, one speculates about who will set the editorial parameters for new virtual publications. How can (or should) we attempt to ensure the "accuracy" of an edition published on a CD-ROM or circulated over the Internet? How will the global nature of today's audience influence both the work of traditional printing and the emerging markets for virtual publications? What role might a reader assume in annotating a computer edition of an author, whether ancient or modern? How might a user of a virtual edition intervene to add digitized images and computer-aided designs to enhance a text? What will the "book" of tomorrow look like? Will it be the computer itself, the software, the personalized web site? How shall we compare in the next millennium the early printers of the fifteenth and sixteenth centuries with today's computer entrepreneurs from the United States, Japan, and from around the world?

Gutenberg's achievements began one of the great revolutions of modern history that will continue unabated into the twenty-first century—a revolution that inspires us to reexamine the innovations of the past in order to comprehend better the possibilities and uncharted technology of the future.

Catalog to
the Exhibition

A Note on Citations

Citations for the incunables have been provided by Paul Needham (with occasional insertions by Michael Joseph, as noted); citations for all other materials have been prepared by Michael Joseph (with occasional insertions by Paul Needham, as noted). For every book in the exhibition there is a reference, given in abbreviation, to a standard bibliography. Abbreviations can be found in the Key to Abbreviations following the list of works cited at the end of the catalog. While all descriptions indicate book format (i.e., the number of folds in the average sheet used for that particular book), the descriptions of the incunables include both format and paper sizes. The nomenclature of the paper sizes is that given by Paul Needham, "Aldus Manutius's Paper Stocks: The Evidence of Two Uncut Books," *Princeton University Library Chronicle* 55 no. 2 (Winter 1994): 287-307.

Library Gallery

Prefatory: [Print 1] DePol, John.
Johann Gutenberg at his Press. July 25, 1986.
Wood engraving. 14.8 x 10.4 cm.
Edition of 110 copies.

Artist's imaginary reconstruction.

1. *[Leaf 1] Biblia Latina.* [Mainz: Johann Gutenberg and Johann Fust, ca. 1454–1455]. Royal F^0.

A single leaf of the Gutenberg Bible, the first major work of European typography. We do not know the close details of Gutenberg's invention of the process of printing texts from multiple cast, reusable characters, but it is very probable that by the early 1450s in Mainz he was producing relatively brief books printed by this technology—in particular, the widely used schoolbook of Latin grammar, the *Ars minor* of Donatus. These earliest experiments survive only in fragments. The much more ambitious project of producing a complete Latin Bible was undertaken with heavy financial support from a Mainz goldsmith, Johann Fust. The date of completion is not certain, but we know that work was far advanced in October 1454, when the future Pope Pius II examined quires of it in Frankfurt, and remarked on its high quality— a judgment with which modern eyes entirely agree. About 180 copies were produced, of which about 40 were on vellum and the remainder on paper. Many copies were sold in the Mainz region, but others were widely distributed in international trade, as far afield as England and Sweden.

Today, about forty-eight integral copies survive, of which some are textually complete with 641 leaves, and others are defective, with losses ranging from a missing leaf or two, to the fragmentary state of the most recently discovered copy, in the church library of Rendsburg, Schleswig-Holstein. Although the Rendsburg copy preserves the first volume of its original binding, the contents of the volume amount to only 131 leaves. Still other copies of the Gutenberg Bible are represented only by scattered fragments preserved as waste material in later bookbindings. These have not been fully identified, copy by copy, but they come from at least twenty other copies, both vellum and paper.

The present leaf comes from an imperfect copy, formerly in the Bavarian State Library, which was acquired in the nineteenth century by the famous book collector and travel writer Robert Curzon, and was sold at Sotheby's in 1920 by his descendants. It was bought by the New York bookdealer Gabriel Wells, who broke it up for sale as single leaves or groups of leaves; thus, the complete book of Genesis from this copy is now in the University of Illinois, the Gospel of Matthew is at Colgate University, etc. The present leaf, with the beginning of 2 Samuel (2 Kings by the Vulgate Bible's nomenclature) is an unusually good example, with its large hand-drawn initial. The Gutenberg Bible did not have printed initial letters: these had to be supplied by hand, as did book and prologue headings, headline titles, and chapter numbers. Each original purchaser commissioned this work of rubrication and/or illumination separately, and some copies were much more elaborately decorated than others. No two copies of the Gutenberg Bible are quite identical in their rubrication, though a few artisan's shops have been identified that worked on more than one copy. The "Noble Fragment" copy is simply but professionally rubricated. Other copies, for example the vellum copy in the Berlin State Library, were very luxuriously illuminated, with gilt initials and elaborate borders.

Reference: Goff B-526

Loaned by Princeton University Library, Department of Rare Books and Special Collections: volume I, leaf 147 (15/9)

2. Gerson, Johannes (1363–1429).
Opusculum tripartitum de praeceptis Decalogi, de confessione, et de arte moriendi. [Cologne: Ulrich Zel, ca. 1467]. Chancery 4⁰.

THE EARLIEST PRINTED BOOK IN THE RUTGERS UNIVERSITY LIBRARIES

Shortly after the completion of the Gutenberg Bible, Johann Fust broke his partnership with Gutenberg and worked independently with Peter Schoeffer. Their first great production was the Mainz Psalter, completed 14 August 1457, and in the following years their shop was notably active. A variety of indirect evidences make it very likely that the first printer of Cologne, Ulrich Zel of Hanau, learned the printing arts in the shop of Fust and Schoeffer. He may have left Mainz in the wake of the "Cathedral War" between two contestants for the see of Mainz. The invasion of the city in October 1462 by the mercenaries of the winning contestant, Prince Adolf of Nassau, left Mainz's civic life in disruption for several years, as many of its leading citizens were forced into exile. Zel matriculated at the University of Cologne in June 1464, and his first dated book belongs to 1466, though it probably had undated predecessors. His type font is essentially a copy of the beautiful and influential font that Fust and Schoeffer used for the Latin Bible of 1462.

Apart from four editions of Cicero's writings, almost all of Zel's publications in his first years were theological tracts aimed at the numerous clergy of

Entry 2, Figure 1.
Gerson, Johannes (1363–1429).
Opusculum tripartitum de praeceptis Decalogi, de confessione, et de arte moriendi.
[Cologne: Ulrich Zel, ca.1467]
Actual size of text block 13.0 x 8.0 cm.

Cologne and its region: St. Augustine, St. John Chrysostom, and, most heavily, Jean Gerson, chancellor of the University of Paris, the noted spiritual author and conciliarist reformer.

Reference: GOFF G-238

The Rutgers copy, formerly owned by the noted collector of incunabula George Dunn, was presented to the Library by the prominent New York bookdealer John F. Fleming.

3. Crescentiis, Petrus de (ca. 1233–ca. 1320).
   Ruralia commoda. [Speyer: Peter Drach, c. 1492].
   Chancery F^0.

Peter Drach, scion of a patrician family of Speyer, established a printing shop there about 1475, and continued printing and publishing into the early sixteenth century. In the 1480s and 1490s he was one of the most active and enterprising of German printer-publishers, second to Koberger in Nuremberg, but to few or no others. His edition of the *Ruralia commoda* of Crescentiis (Piero de' Crescenzi) was his most ambitious illustrated edition, for which he commissioned nearly 290 column-width woodcuts, using them both in this Latin edition, and in German-language editions of 1 October 1493 and of ca. 1495. Drach's editions of Crescentiis were the most heavily illustrated of those printed in the fifteenth century. The woodcuts of agriculture occupations and of hunting are derived from the manuscript tradition of the *Ruralia commoda.* The numerous woodcuts of plants and herbs are copied from illustrations of the *Hortus sanitatis,* a massive herbal published in Mainz by Jacob Meydenbach, 23 June 1491 (Goff H–486).

Reference: Goff C–969

4. Schedel, Hartmann (1440–1514).
   Liber cronicarum.
   Augsburg: Johann Schönsperger, 1 February 1497.
   Chancery F^0.

The *Liber cronicarum* or Nuremberg Chronicle, as it
is commonly called, was first printed in Nuremberg
by Anton Koberger in 1493, in both Latin and German editions. It was compiled from a wide variety of
sources by Hartmann Schedel, a wealthy and scholarly
Nuremberg physician, and was provided with an
extraordinary range of woodcut illustration, ranging
from double-page city views to small vignettes and
decorative linking blocks. The illustrations were commissioned from the workshop of the Nuremberg
artists Michael Wolgemut and Hans Pleydenwurff, the
shop where Albrecht Dürer had shortly before served
an apprenticeship. Koberger's two editions, printed on
the largest (Imperial) paper, are, in terms of their com-
plicated intermingling of typographic text and woodcuts, the most complex examples of printing in the
fifteenth century. Copies were distributed to many
cities in Europe, including to Italy and Spain; cus-
tomers could acquire them either hand-colored or,
more cheaply, uncolored. But even uncolored, it was
a very expensive book.

The prolific Augsburg printer Johann Schönsperger
saw that there could be a market for a less-expensive
version of the Nuremberg Chronicle. Probably without Koberger's permission, he reprinted the Nuremberg Chronicle on ordinary-size (Chancery) paper,
with woodcuts copied from those of the Nuremberg
editions. The number of woodcuts was considerably
reduced, but all the same they would have represented
a considerable cost for Schönsperger. He printed
editions both in German (18 September 1496) and, as
here, in Latin (1497). The German edition certainly
sold out, for he reprinted it a second time in 1500.

The Rutgers copy came as the gift of the eminent
geologist, John Conover Smock (1842–1926).

Reference: Goff S–308

5. Josephus, Flavius.

[Opera, German, tr. Caspar Hedion:] *Josephi… Zwentzig bücher von den alten geschichten*. Strassburg: Balthasar Beck, May 1535. F⁰.

The German edition of Josephus's *Works* was retranslated from Erasmus's Latin translation and printed by Balthassar Beck in Strassburg in 1535. Despite their many imperfections, which include, not insignificantly, their dubious value as history, and the intrusive vamping of the author, the writings of Flavius Josephus (37/38–ca. 100) on the Jewish revolt of 66–70 and on earlier Jewish history do shed an invaluable light on the mentality of subject peoples under the Roman Empire. The printer, Balthassar Beck (fl. 1525–1552), employs a *bâtarde* typeface—a name given to vernacular, or regional, typefaces based upon scribal paradigms in which speed of composition replaced formality (see also #29, 30); the most remarkable feature of Beck's type is its grotesque Fraktur capitals (see also #27).

The Rutgers copy bound in quarter sheep with pattern paper end sheets; *provenance*: ex libris Dr. George Kloss (1787–1854); nineteenth-century manuscript signatures of Michael Gamel and Joannis Gross [Johann Friedrich Gross? (1732–1795)].

Reference: VD16 J970
Reference: Goff J-485

Entry 5, Figure 2.
Josephus, Flavius.
Josephi, Zwentzig bücher von den alten geschichten.
Strassburg: [Balthassar Beck], 1535.
Actual size of block 6.0 x 5.8 cm.

6. *[Print 2]* Dürer, Albrecht (1471–1528).
   St. Jerome in His Cell. 1511.
   Wood relief.
   Loaned by the Zimmerli Art Museum.
   Gift of the Estate of
   Raymond V. Carpenter, ZAM #054.

7. *[Print 3]* Dürer, Albrecht (1471–1528).
   Virgin with a Pear. 1511.
   Engraving.
   Loaned by the Zimmerli Art Museum.
   Gift of the Estate of
   Raymond V. Carpenter, ZAM #0540.

8. Rainerius de Pisis (fl. 1330–1347,
   d. ca. 1351).
   *Pantheologia, sive, Summa
   universae theologiae.*
   [Augsburg: Günther Zainer], 1474.
   Royal F⁰.

Entry 8, Figure 3.
Rainerus de Pisis, (fl. 1330–1347, d. ca. 1351).
Pantheologia, sive, Summa universae theologiae.
[Augsburg: Günther Zainer], 1474.
Actual size of block 4.0 x 3.9 cm.

Günther Zainer, a native of Reutlingen, established himself in 1468 as the first printer of Augsburg, an Imperial free city which became, alongside Strassburg and Nuremberg, one of the trio of great printing towns of southern Germany. From 1468 to 1477, Zainer was perhaps the most active and diversified printer in Germany. He issued both Latin and German texts, ranging in size from the *Pantheologia* shown here to single-leaf calendars. From 1471, many of his works were illustrated with woodcut series, and others, whose texts did not call for illustration, with attractive woodcut initials. Zainer introduced Roman types to Germany (late 1471), stating in his first use of them that he ceded nothing to the Italians. He died 13 April 1478.

Entry 9, Figure 4.
Biblia Latina.
[Ulm: Johann Zainer],
29 Jan. (IV Kal. Feb.) 1480.
Actual size of block 4.5 x 4.2 cm.

The *Pantheologia* is an alphabetical summation of theology. Its author, Rainerius of Pisa, was a Dominican; we know from an authorial prologue that he began his giant work in 1333. The early printed editions add to the *Pantheologia* proper an extensive table, composed in the early 1460s by one Jacobus Florentinus, a Franciscan, and dedicated by him to the eminent Dominican cardinal, Johannes de Turrecremata (d. 1468). The *Pantheologia* is a good example of the revivifying effects of typography. It does not survive in a large number of manuscripts compared with many other theological *Summae,* but courtesy of the printing shops it came to enjoy a vigorous second life, more than a century after it was first issued. Six editions were printed between 1473 and 1486, five in Germany and one in Venice, after which the text fell into abeyance again.

Günther Zainer's edition was the second, copied from the Nuremberg *editio princeps* of 8 April 1473.

Reference: Goff R–6

Loaned by Leonard Hansen, Class of '43

9. *Biblia Latina.*
[Ulm: Johann Zainer],
29 Jan. 1480. Royal F⁰.

Johann Zainer, the first printer of Ulm (1473), was the brother of Günther Zainer, first printer of Augsburg (see #8). Both learned the printing trade in Strassburg, and both moved then to Augsburg. It is presumed but not certain that Johann worked in the shop of

his elder brother before setting up on his own in the
smaller city of Ulm, 65 km west of Augsburg. As with
Günther Zainer, many of Johann's editions are distinguished by fine illustration woodcuts, initials, and bor-
derpieces. His 1480 Bible in Latin, with its striking
"rococo-alphabet" initials, was one of his two most
substantial editions. The only Latin Bible printed in
Augsburg or Ulm in the fifteenth century, it is also
among the most beautiful of all early printed Bibles.
After 1480 plain-text Latin Bibles stopped being
produced in the lectern-size Royal folio format, in
favor of more compendious and, eventually, even
portable formats.

Reference: Goff B-567
Loaned by Leonard Hansen, Class of '43

10. Reisch, Gregor (d.1525).
    Margarita philosophica.
    [Freiburg im Breisgau]: Johann Schott,
    16 March 1504. 4⁰.

Written for young people, the *Margarita philosophica*
covers the whole course of university study in its time,
including the *trivium* and *quadrivium*. The generally
unexcitable Encyclopedia Britannica (15th ed.) pro-
claims it "one of the most delightful of all encyclope-
dias" (EB 18:272, 2b).
   It was printed by Johann Grüninger after the earlier
edition (before 13 July 1503) of Johann Schott, with
woodcuts copied from Schott's. Johann Schott
(1477–1548) was the son of a printer, Martin Schott
(d.1499)—son-in-law of the first printer of Strassburg,
Johann Mentelin—and one of the most active of early
Strassburg printers. Among the city's artists employed
by Schott who conceivably contributed to the
Margarita philosophica were Hans Schäuffelein, Hans
Baldung (d. 1545), Hans Weiditz (see #12), and
Johann Wechtlin.

References: Adams R333; VD16 R1035

11. Valla, Lorenzo (1406–1457).
Laurentii Vallae Elegantiarum libri sex.
Mainz: Johan Schöffer, December 1522. 8⁰.

Lorenzo Valla (1406–1457) was an Italian humanist, philosopher, and literary critic of surprising originality and strength. Born in Rome, Valla's first published work was a defense of a life of prudent erotic pleasure, in which he critiqued certain touchstones of orthodoxy, such as a belief in the superiority of stoic virtue and the contemplative life (see #3). In later, more mature, works he attacked the *Poetics* of Aristotle and Cicero's speeches, finding time to engage in published disputes with his much regarded contemporaries, such as Poggio Bracciolini (1380–1459). One contemporary drily observed, Valla wrote simply to disturb people—a comment that, if true to his critical spirit, unfairly minimizes Valla's substantial contribution to the consolidation of Italian and Northern humanism (Kristeller, 35).

Valla's *Elegantiae linguae latinae* (published in 1444 and first printed in 1471) was the first textbook of Latin grammar, phraseology, and style to be written since late antiquity, and in its preface, Valla boasts of his noble intention to "restore the Latin language to the glory and purity that marked it before its corruption by the barbarians" (Garin, 600). Paul Kristeller regards Valla's grammar as a "major effort in the history of humanist philology" (Kristeller, 25), and notes that it remained highly popular in grammar schools all over Europe down to the early nineteenth century (see #48 for comparison).

The printer, Johann Schöffer of Mainz, was the son of Peter Schöffer (ca. 1425–ca. 1502), a calligrapher, who assisted Gutenberg in his preparation of the printing of the forty-two-line Bible (see #1), and under Gutenberg's supervision, designed the first typeface. After Gutenberg's bankruptcy, Schöffer continued as a printer, financed by Johann Fust (1400–1466). Among his historically significant publications is the so-called Mainz Psalter of 1457 (*Psalterium. With canticles, hymns, capitula, preces maiores and minores.*

[Mainz], Johann Fust and Peter Schoeffer, 14 August 1457), the first book to integrate multiple colored inks in the same press run. Johann Schöffer took over the business from his father in 1503, and remained unofficial printer to the university until 1531. Most of his books are of classical scholarship. Historians reference his 1505 German translation of Livy in fortifying the case for Gutenberg as the inventor of printing from types, remarking in its colophon the following passage: "In Mainz the ingenious Johann Gutenberg invented the wonderful art of printing in the year 1450, after which it was improved and finished by the industry, expenses, and labor of Johannes Fust and Peter Schöffer in Mainz." The large rococo initials in his edition of Valla may have been designed by Conrad Faber von Creuznach (1500?–1533), or Gabriel Zehender, two artists associated with his shop.

References: Adams V168; VD16 V237

12. Brunfels, Otto (1488–1534). (See color plate, page 50)
    Herbarum vivae eicones ad nature imitationem.
    Strassburg: Johann Schott, 1530. F^0.

The inadequacies of Otto Brunfels' derivative text are redeemed by the beauty and historic importance of its illustration which makes the *Herbarum vivae eicones* one of the two unrivaled masterpieces of the Germanic school of exact realism, and an exemplar of subtlety, accuracy, and elegance. Brunfels' botanical pastiche crowned a varied career as the town physician at Bern, a pastor and a sometime naturalist. Brunfels and Johann Schott, the book's publisher (see also #10), were very close colleagues, owing to common sympathies with the Reformation, and Schott was probably the prime mover behind the production of *Herbarum vivae eicones* (Rytz, 18–21), with Brunfels a willing hand. The illustrations and delicately carved woodcuts are by Hans Weiditz (fl. 1475–1518), a remarkable draftsman and block cutter. His style matured during his late teens in the service of Hans Bargkmair in Augsburg, and in part reveals the influence of Albrecht

Dürer. In *Herbarum vivae eicones*, Weiditz gives us the first botanical studies of the Renaissance that are properly scientific in their concern for descriptive accuracy and comprehensiveness.

C.P. Snow's famous dictum, that art and science constitute separate cultures, might once have seemed less self-evident: printed and illustrated herbals like Brunfels' actually caused the study of herbal medicine to dominate theurapeutics for a century and a half (Stannard, 212–220).

References: Adams B2923; VD16 B8499

13. Dioscorides, Pedanius. (See color plate, page 51)
De medicinali materia libri sex, Ioanne Rvellio Svessionensi interprete.
Frankfurt am Main: Christian Egenolph, April 1549. F^0.

Printed in Frankfurt by Christian Egenolph in 1549, the *Peri hylēs iatrikēs* of Pedanius Dioscorides of Anazarbos, commonly called *Materia medica*, was the first authoritative botanic work of antiquity, and Dioscorides the first to categorize medical botany as an applied science. It remained the standard work until the eighteenth century, and of the 600 plants it describes with their medical properties, 90 are still in use today. The sixth book comprises the *De venenis* and the *De venenatis animalibus*, which in the original edition of this translation (1516) was divided into four books numbered six to nine. The *Notha* and *Adscripta* are not printed in this edition.

In 1486, the Imperial city of Frankfurt gained the dubious distinction of erecting the first secular censorship office. Despite the persistence of secular censorship within its walls, however, following the arrival of Sigmund Feyerabend in 1528, and Christian Egenolph in 1530, Frankfurt grew to achieve an international reputation for the production and marketing of types. The large number of books issued by Feyerabend's press helped to make Fraktur type, to which he was stoutly committed, the national type of Germany (just as Roman was becoming the national type of Italy).

Egenolph's type foundry, established in 1531, rose to become the most influential firm in the seventeenth century. Even in the eighteenth century, under the new name of *Luther*, it sold its manufacture as far as Philadelphia where the first American foundry, established in 1772, became its customer.

Egenolph's publications are distinguished by the beauty of their woodcut illustrations, for which Frankfurt also secured an international reputation during the second half of the sixteenth century.

References: Adams D664; VD16 D2005

14. Jacobus de Voragine (ca. 1228/29–1298).
Legenda aurea sanctorum, sive Lombardica historia.
Cologne: Conrad Winters, de Homborch, 1481.
Chancery F⁰.

Conrad Winters, a native of Hamburg, had an active printing shop in Cologne from ca. 1475 to 1482, which primarily served the reading needs of the numerous clergy of the archdiocese, both regular and secular. This is the latest of four editions Winters printed of the *Legenda aurea* or *Golden Legend* composed by Jacobus de Voragine, the Dominican Archbishop of Genoa. The work is a collection of saints' lives arranged calendrically by feast days. It was continuously popular from the late thirteenth to early sixteenth centuries. More than seventy Latin editions of the *Golden Legend* were printed in the fifteenth century; and nearly eighty editions, often with woodcut illustrations of the saints, were printed variously in Catalan, Czech, Dutch, English (translated by William Caxton), French, Low and High German, Italian, and Spanish. An acquaintance with the *Golden Legend* is indispensable for understanding the common religious mind in Europe in the later Middle Ages.

This copy stayed in the region of Cologne for centuries. It retains its original binding from that area, and in the eighteenth century belonged to the Benedictine monastery of St. Nicholas in Brauweiler, near

Cologne. After that monastery was dissolved, it was acquired by Dr. Georg Kloss, a physician of Frankfurt, whose enormous collection of incunables was sold at Sotheby's in London, 1835.

Reference: Goff J–98

Loaned by Leonard Hansen, Class of '43

Printing in Italy

15. *[Leaf 2]* Nicolaus de Lyra (ca. 1270–1340).
Postilla super totam bibliam.
[Rome: Conrad Sweynheym
& Arnold Pannartz, 1471]. Royal F^0.

Conrad Sweynheym and Arnold Pannartz are widely accepted as the first to bring typography to Italy, where the new art soon flourished even more strongly than in Germany. Sweynheym was a cleric of Mainz, and it is likely that he and Pannartz migrated to Italy in the aftermath of the Mainz Cathedral War of 1462 (see #1). Their first printing shop (1465) was in the ancient monastery of Subiaco, 70 km east of Rome — the cradle house of the Benedictine order. In the course of 1467, they moved to Rome, where over the next five years they undertook an ambitious program of editions of classical texts and church fathers, spaciously laid out and printed with a fine Roman (antiqua) type. Their production overran their market, and reached a crisis as they produced a five-volume edition of the giant Bible commentary of the Franciscan Biblical scholar Nicolaus de Lyra. The last volume of the Lyra contains an appeal for financial aid to Pope Sixtus IV, to which is joined a list of thirty-seven editions printed to date by Sweynheym and Pannartz.

It appears that they were at least partly successful in their petition, being granted several ecclesiastical benefices. Their printing partnership continued into the spring of 1473, after which Sweynheym disappears from historical record. Pannartz continued to print on his own in 1474 and after.

Reference: Goff N–131

16. Suetonius (b. ca. A.D. 69). (See color plate, page 52)
    Vitae XII Caesarum.
    [Venice]: Nicolas Jenson, [first half of] 1471. Royal 4⁰.

Nicolas Jenson (birthdate unknown, d. fall of 1480) stands alongside Gutenberg, Caxton, and Aldus Manutius as one of a select group of fifteenth-century printers whose names still enjoy a wide general recognition. Jenson was a native of Sommevoire, near Troyes. He first appears to public view as a printer in Venice, 1470, but there is a plausible, though not fully authenticated, record of the French mint stating that in the fall of 1458 he had been sent to Mainz by King Charles VIII, to learn the arts of printing and bring the knowledge back to France. It is noteworthy that in his Venice years, Jenson had close business connections with several German merchants. Jenson's chief article of fame is the beautiful Roman font he designed, shown to good advantage in the present volume. The opening, displayed where Jenson's font is complemented by a beautifully drawn faceted initial G in the manner of the best Roman inscriptions, is an example of perfect book design.

Jenson's Roman font was famous both in its own day and today. But it should be recalled that he also designed several rotunda Gothic fonts for law printing that were likewise highly influential, and were for their purpose equal in quality to his Roman.

Reference: Goff S-817

17. Antoninus Florentinus (1389–1459; Saint;
    Archbishop of Florence from 1446).
    (See color plate, page 53)
    De Censuris.
    [Mantua: Paulus de Butzbach, ca. 1475]. Median 4^0.

Paulus de Butzbach (in Hesse, 35 km north of Frankfurt am Main) is a good representative of the numer
ous clan of Germans who come to light in the early
printing trade of Italy. He apparently first worked as a
printer in Verona, ca. 1471–72, in partnership with a
Georgius de Augusta (Augsburg). In late 1471 he and
Georgius entered into a contract to print in Mantua
for a doctor of laws there, Peter Adam de Michaelibus.
The chief claim to fame of Paulus and Georgius is
their joint colophon in the 1472 Mantua edition of
Dante's *Commedia* (Goff D–23), one of three editions
of the *Commedia* appearing that year. From that point
Georgius de Augusta disappears from view, but
Butzbach continued printing in Mantua to 1481.

Butzbach's edition of *De Censuris* is an extract from
the large *Summa* of moral theology of the Dominican
scholar-saint Antonino Pierozzi (canonized 1523), the
most important religious figure of Florence in the
generation before Savonarola and a man much loved
by the poor of the city. In the first decades of printing,
more than 140 editions of various of Antoninus's writings were published, ranging in extent from brief
tracts and many editions of his various confessional
guides, to his giant world chronicle, and his
Summa theologica.

The Rutgers copy bound in early calf over wooden
boards, rebacked, with headbands and speckled text
edges; acquired for the Libraries through the Julia
Williamson Fund, 796408; one of five in the United
States *(–mj).*

Reference: Goff A–775

18. Dante Alighieri (1265–1321).
La Commedia (with commentary of Cristoforo Landino). Venice: Petrus de Quarengiis, 11 October 1497. Chancery F⁰.

Fifteen editions of Dante's *Divine Comedy* were printed in the fifteenth century. From the 30 August 1481 Florence edition onward, they all included the commentary of the Florentine scholar Cristoforo Landino. The 1481 Dante (Goff D-29) was intended to be fully illustrated with beautiful engravings based on drawings of Botticelli, but the project was abortive: engravings were made only for the first nineteen cantos of *Inferno*, and only a small fraction of the surviving copies contain these engravings. A Brescia edition of 31 May 1487 (D-31) was illustrated with full-page woodcuts, but likewise incompletely: the series of illustrations ended with canto 1 of *Paradiso*. The first fully illustrated Dante was printed in Venice by Bernardinus Benalius and Matteo Capcasa, 3 March 1491 (D-32), with vignette (column-width) cuts for the cantos, and full-page cuts introducing *Inferno*, *Purgatorio*, and *Paradiso*. Their artist has been convincingly identified by Professor Lillian Armstrong as the "Pico Master," a still-nameless but important figure whose work is found both in illuminated manuscripts, and in woodcut designs for Venetian printers.

The 1491 Dante woodcuts were reused by Capcasa in his 29 November 1493 edition (D-33), and in this

Entry 18, Figure 5.
Dante Alighieri (1265–1321).
La Commedia.
Venice: Petrus de Quarengiis, 11 October 1497.
Actual size of block 8.3 x 8.4 cm.

edition by Quarengiis, 1497. The woodblocks remained in Venice, and were used again by Bartolommeo Zani in his 1507 Dante.

The Rutgers copy contains the ownership inscription of "Elizabeth Lecky Wood, Rome, 1870"—a place and time when, one imagines, almost every little antique shop might have a few incunables lying about. Presented to the Libraries by E. Byrne Hackett, Esq. (b. 1879); 212695.

Reference: Goff D–35

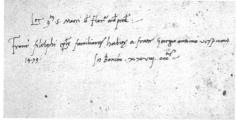

Entry 19, Figures 6 and 7.
Filelfo, Francesco (1398–1481).
[Epistolae.]
[Venice: Vindelinus de Spira, 1473]

19. Filelfo, Francesco (1398–1481).
    Epistolae.
    [Venice: Vindelinus de Spira, before 6 October 1473]. Chancery F^0.

FIRST EDITION. This collection of letters written by Filelfo (Latin, Philelphus) between 1427 and 1461 is one of the first substantial publications of a living humanist author. Although the edition is undated, Filelfo referred to it as recently published in a letter he wrote to a friend on 6 October 1473. The collection became popular as a model of Latin prose. About twenty more editions appeared before the end of the century, either complete or in abridged versions for school use. The printer Vindelinus de Spira, with whom Filelfo was acquainted, succeeded his brother Johannes de Spira as head of the first printing shop in Venice (1469). In September 1469

Johannes had obtained from the Venetian senate a
five-year monopoly for printing in Venice, but his
death shortly afterward voided the privilege, and over
the years 1470–1472 about fifteen more printing
shops opened in Venice—though many of these
folded up again in short order.

The Rutgers copy of Filelfo's *Epistolae* is of great
interest for its early ownerships. It was first acquired by
the Florentine ecclesiastic Giorgio Antonio Vespucci
(ca. 1434–1514), who had a high reputation for the
humanist school he led. Among his pupils was his
nephew Amerigo Vespucci, the explorer and travel
writer whose name became attached, in the first
decade of the sixteenth century, to the two new conti-
nents of North and South America. In 1499 Vespucci
entered the Dominican convent of San Marco. He
donated the major part of his extensive library of
manuscripts and incunables, including this volume, to
the convent's famed library, which was a chief resort of
Florentine humanists. The volume contains Vespucci's
autograph inscription, extensive red-ink marginalia
apparently in his hand, and the acquisition note and
shelfmark of San Marco: *"a fratre Georgio antonio
vespuccio 1499. In bancha xxviij occidentalis."* Many of
Vespucci's books are still preserved in the Biblioteca
Nazionale and the Biblioteca Mediceo-Laurenziano in
Florence. The Rutgers volume is one of only a hand-
ful known outside of Florence.

Reference: Goff P-583

20. *[Leaf 3]* Gastaldi, Giacomo.
     Tierra Nueva.
     [Venice: Gioä Baptista Pedrazzano, 1548].
     Copperplate engraving, 130 x 175 mm.

The first regional map of the east coast of North
America: from Ptolemy's *La Geografia*. This edition
was the most comprehensive atlas produced between
Martin Waldseemüller's *Geographiae* of 1513, and the
Abraham Ortelius *Theatrum* of 1570, and the first to

contain regional maps of the American continent. Giacomo Gastaldi had the maps beautifully engraved on copper, which marked a turning point in the history of map production: from now on the majority of maps preferred copper over wood since its hardness gave the engraver the ability to render greater detail.

21. [Julius Pomponius Laetus (1428–1498)].
Columellae Hortuli commentarium.
[Rome: Bartholomaeus Guldinbeck, ca. 1485].
Chancery 4⁰.

The *De re rustica* of Columella (fl. ca. 36–65 A.D.), in twelve books, was the most comprehensive of the classical Roman treatises on agriculture. As a complete text, it was printed in the incunable period together with other treatises of Cato the Censor, Varro, and Palladius as a collective *Scriptores rei rusticae* or *Opera agricolationum* (Venice: Jenson, 1472 and subsequent editions). Book X of Columella, on gardens, which was written in hexameter verses rather than the prose of the remaining books, also had an independent and self-standing popularity. Besides the five incunable editions of *Scriptores rei rusticae*, there were seven brief editions of Book X, *De cultu hortorum*. The present edition, although treated in incunable catalogs as a work of Columella, is in fact a Renaissance commentary on Book X, composed by the Roman humanist Pomponius Laetus, and completed by him in 1467 or before. Pomponius's commentary is known in two versions, a fuller one with his name given, and a shorter one (as here) without his name. The full version was first printed as surrounding commentary to an edition Columella Book X (Goff C–764, Venice, ca. 1481), and then from 1494 onward it was included regularly in editions of *Scriptores rei rusticae*. The shorter, anonymous version was separately printed in three Rome editions between ca. 1471 and ca. 1490, this being the second of the three. These separate editions, probably

intended for local school use, are quite rare; the first
edition is not represented in America, and this is the
only American copy of the second.

Reference: Goff C-765

22. Cicero, Marcus Tullius (106−43 B.C.).
    Epistolae elegantiores.
    [Rome: Bartholomaeus Guldinbeck, 1485].
    Chancery 4⁰.

Cicero, who was taken to define the standard of Latin
prose, was (excluding the school grammar of Donatus)
the most widely printed classical author in the incunable period. More than 330 fifteenth-century editions
of his writings survive, from a collected *Opera* (Milan,
1498–99) to many dozens of smaller collections and
individual works. The present collection of 63 selected
letters forms a distinct publishing class among the
many editions of Cicero's letters. It was first printed
in Naples, 1471, with a dedicatory letter from Petrus
Bartolacius of Benevento to one Alvarus de Cosman
(Guzman?), perhaps his noble pupil. Twelve further
incunable editions followed, dropping the dedication
of Bartolacius: ten containing the letters alone, and
two more with a commentary by Martinus Phileticus.
All these were printed in Naples or Rome. It is curi-
ous to note, however, that sales were far from local.
Most of the printers were Germans, and they clearly
maintained trade connections with their native land,
leading to wide distribution of copies north of the
Alps. Today, of the total of 13 editions—all rare—
only 5 are represented in Italian libraries, and more
copies are known having early German ownership
indications than Italian.

The Rutgers copy, one of three known (the others in
Rome and Lausanne), was formerly owned by George
Dunn and C. W. Clark, and was presented to Rutgers
by the late New York bookdealer John F. Fleming.

Reference: Goff C-538

Entry 24, Figure 8.
Origenes.
[In Evangelium Ioannis Explanationum.]
Venice: Andrea & Giacomo Spinelli, 1551.
Actual size of block 4.8 x 4.1 cm.

23. Maffeus, Celsus (1425–1508).
Monumentum compendiosum pro confessionibus cardinalium et prelatorum.
Venice: Petrus de Quarengiis,
22 March 1498. Chancery 4^0.

Celsi Maffei was a member of a prominent family of Verona, a number of whose members rose to significant positions within the Italian church. He was the prior of the Augustinian house of San Giovanni Battista in Verdara, outside Padua, and served repeatedly as General of the reformed Lateran Congregation of Augustinians. He wrote a number of brief works published in his lifetime, including a defense of the dignity of the Canons Regular against that of the monastic orders. This is the latest of four incunable editions of Maffei's brief tract (in his colophon he called it a *Scrutatoriolum,* or "little examination book") on hearing confessions from cardinals and other prelates of the church.

A dozen copies of this edition are recorded in Italian libraries, including three in Verona, but the Rutgers copy is the only one in America.

Reference: Goff (Suppl.) M–19a

24. Origenes.
In Evangelium Ioannis Explanationum, tomi xxxii.
Venice: Andrea & Giacomo Spinelli,
1551. 4^0.

A figure of considerable learning, a dedicated pedagogue and a person of powerful intellectual energies, Origenes, var., Origenis Adamantius,

of Alexandria (ca. 184–ca. 253), was the most important theologian and Biblical scholar of the early Greek
Church. However, colorful beliefs (his hypothesis of
the preexistence of souls, for example) severely
damaged his posthumous reputation. *In Evangelium
Ioannis Explanationum*, printed in Venice by Andrea
(fl. 1549–1555) and Giacomo Spinelli (fl. 1551–1555),
in 1551, forms a part of the beginning of Origen's
immense commentary on St. John, written to refute
the commentary of the Gnostic followers of the
Egyptian, Valentinus.

The Rutgers copy from W.R.H. Jeudwine, with
his ex libris.

Reference: BN v.127, c2130
Loaned by Leonard Hansen, Class of '43

25-6. Homer. *Iliad* and *Odyssey, Greek* (with pseudo-
Homer, *Batrachomyomachia*, and the Homeric
Hymns). Florence: Demetrius Damilas, for Bernar-
dus and Nerius Nerlius and Giovanni Acciaiuoli,
9 December 1488 [but shortly after 13 January
1488/89]. Median F^0.

FIRST EDITION. The *editio princeps* of Homer was the
most ambitious piece of Greek printing until Aldus
Manutius's five-volume Aristotle (1495–1498). The
editor was Demetrios Chalcondylas (ca. 1424–1511),
the Athenian-born humanist who taught Greek in
Florence. The Greek font, designed by Demetrius
Damilas of Crete, is a recasting of that used for
the 1476 Milan edition of Constantine Lascaris,
Erotemata (Goff L–65). The colophon date is
9 December 1488. Bernardo Nerli's dedication to
Piero de' Medici is dated 13 January 1488/89, and
was apparently added to the hitherto blank first
page more than a month after the edition proper
was completed.

   The Florentine Homer would have been a
very expensive project; it included a limited issue
printed on vellum. It is doubtful, however, that it

was financially successful. A considerable proportion of the surviving copies bear no signs of use or ownership until the eighteenth century, and it may well be that much of the edition remained in unbound sheets for more than two centuries, at which time many connoisseur collectors of early classical editions finally created a new demand for copies. The Rutgers copy, with initials left blank and in eighteenth century gilt red morocco, seems to exemplify this hypothesis. It belonged at an early time to the British Museum, but was deaccessioned as a duplicate in 1804. It should be noted that the British Museum, now British Library, did not greatly impoverish its holdings in disposing of this copy. Four other copies remain there still, a fifth having been deaccessioned in 1931.

Reference: Goff H-300

27. Josephus, Flavius (A.D. 37/38–c. 100).
(See color plate on page 54)
De antiquitate Judaica; De bello Judaico (transl. pseudo-Rufinus; with a *Vita Josephi* by Hieronymus Squarzaficus). Venice: Reynaldus de Novimagio, 31 March (part I) & 10 May 1481 (part II). Chancery F^0.

Fifth edition, but the first to attribute the translation to Tyrannius Rufinus, contemporary of St. Jerome. A postscript below the colophon by the humanist Hieronymus Squarzaficus (fl. 1471–1503) makes the attribution. Squarzaficus, whose biography is principally known through scattered incunable prefaces, notes in his postscript that he had just returned from travels in Greece when he found that Reynaldus's edition was about to appear, but that it lacked what he immediately supplied, a eulogy and life of Josephus. Rufinus has been accepted in even the best incunable literature as Josephus's translator, but the attribution is both doubtful and incomplete. In the early sixth century, Cassiodorus wrote in his *Institutiones* that the Latin version of Josephus's Jewish War circulated with uncertain attributions to St. Jerome, St. Ambrose, or

Rufinus; and stated that his own friends had translated the *Jewish Antiquities* at this request. Thus, the two translations are separated in time by a century or more.

The printer Reynaldus de Novimagio immigrated to Venice from Nijmegen in Holland, and is recorded as a printer there from 1477 to 1496, though with several years-long gaps in his dated output. He married a Venetian widow, Donna Paola, two of whose three preceding husbands had been German immigrant printers: Johannes de Spira, first printer of Venice, and Johannes de Colonia. The Hellingas have suggested with much plausibility (HPT I, 37) that Reynaldus was also active as a typecutter and -seller. The text type of this *Josephus* appears also in the printing shop of Matthaeus Cerdonis in Padua, and more remarkably, in that of Gerard Leeu in Gouda.

The Rutgers copy is rubricated throughout in red, purple, and blue; the first page is illuminated in the Venetian style, in red, blue, green, magenta, and gold leaf; bound in vellum over boards, with gilt-stamped spine and blue spotted text edges; with annotations in early hand. The Rutgers copy is one of thirteen in United States *(–mj)*.

Reference: Goff J-485

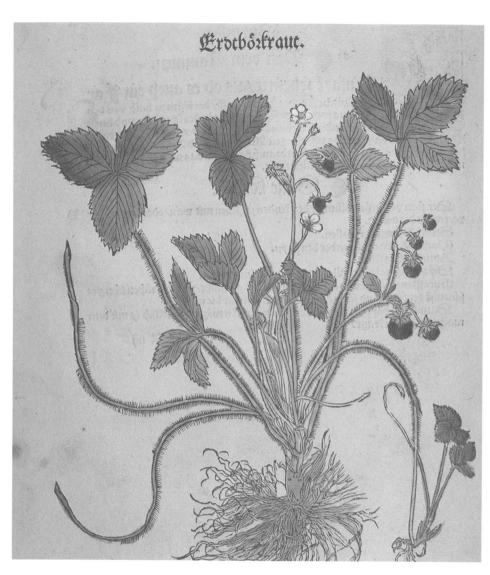

Entry 12, Figure 9.
Otto Brunfels (1488–1534).
Herbarum vivae eicones.
Strassburg: Johann Schott, 1530.
Actual size of block 18.0 x 16.1 cm.

Draco marinus.　　**Caput　XII.**

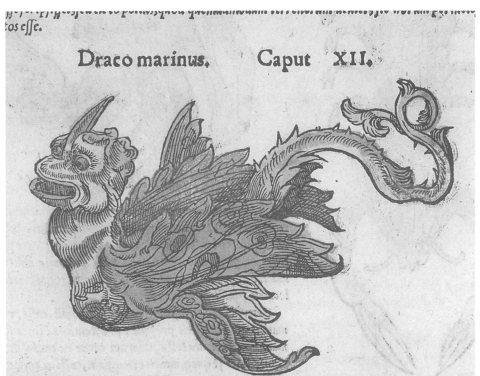

Raco marinus diffectus & apertus impofitus cp,ictus fpinæ fuæ qua fer dela eft.

HO

Entry 13, Figure 10.
Dioscorides, Pedanius.
De medicinali materia.
Frankfurt am Main: Christoph Egenolph, 1549.
Actual size of block 7.2 x 10.5 cm.

51

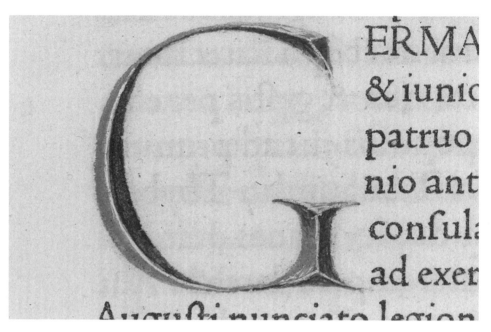

Entry 16, Figure 11.
Suetonius, b.ca. 69.
Vitae XII Caesarum.
[Venice: Nicolas Jenson], 1471.
Actual size of letter 3.4 x 3.4 cm.

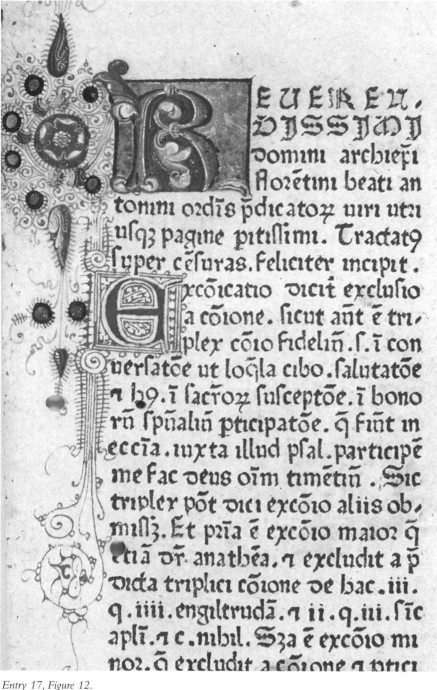

EUEREU. DISSIMI domini archiepi florétini beati antonini ordis pdicatoz uiri utzi ufq3 pagine pitiſſimi. Tractat9 fuper céfuras. feliciter incipit.

Excōicatio dicit excluſio a cōione. ſicut aūt ē triplex cōio fideliū. ſ. ī conuerſatōe ut loqla cibo. ſalutatōe ꝟ h9. ī ſacroz ſuſceptōe. ī bonorū ſpūaliū pticipatōe. ꝙ fiūt in eccīa. iuxta illud pſal. participé me fac deus oīm timétiū. Sīc tripler pōt dici excōio aliis obmiſſz. Et pīa ē excōio maioz ꝙ etiā dr̄ anathēa. ꝯ excludit a p̄ dicta triplici cōione de hac. iii. q. iiii. engiltrudā. ꝯ ii. q. iii. ſīc aplī. ꝯ c. nibil. Sza ē excōio minoz. ꝙ excludit a cōione ꝯ ptici

Entry 17, Figure 12.
Antoninus Florentinus (1389–1459, Saint; Archbishop of Florence from 1446)
De Censuris.
[Mantua: Paulus de Butzbach, ca. 1475]
Actual size of text block 15.0 x 4.4 cm.

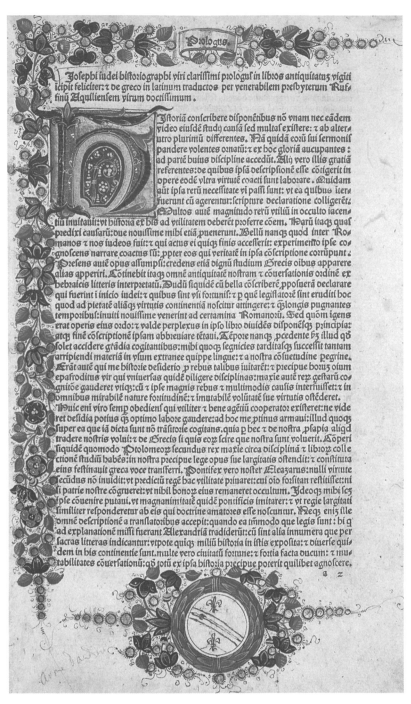

Entry 27, Figure 13.

Josephus, Flavius (A.D. 37/38–c. 100).

De antiquitate Judaica. De bello Judaico.

Venice: Raynaldus de Novimagio, 1481.

Actual size of text block 20.1 x 12.1 cm.

54

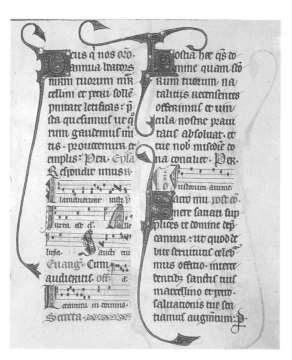

Entry 28, Figures 14 and 15.
French Missal. Beauvais, ca. 1280.
Actual size of leaf 28.6 x 20.0 cm.

Entry 29, Figure 16
[Leaf 7] Schedel, Hartmann (1440–1514).
[Liber chronicarum]. Liber cronicarum.
Nuremberg: Anton Koberger, 1493.
Actual size of block 11.8 x 15.5 cm.

Entry 31, Figure 17.
Jacobus de Voragine (ca. 1230–ca. 1298).
Legenda aurea sanctorum, sive Lombardica historia.
Lyons: Mathias Huss, 1487.
Actual size of block 8.0 x 6.6 cm.

28. *[Leaf 4]* Missal. (See color plate
on page 55)
[Beauvais, ca. 1280.]
Textura in red and black, with
musical notation.

29. *[Leaf 5]* Schedel, Hartmann,
1440–1514.
[Liber chronicarum]. Liber cronicarum.
Nuremberg: Anton Koberger, 1493.
(See #4, #A1.)

30. *[Leaf 6]* Bible. *German.* 1483.
[Nuremburg: Anton Koberger, 1483].

Hand-colored woodcut illustration
from the Book of Exodus. The illustrations for Anton Koberger's German
Bible were previously used for the
Cologne edition of the Bible published by Heinrich Quentell (d. 1501)
in 1480 (see also #53). Of the German
dialect Koberger used, Luther is
reputed to have said, "no one could
speak German of this outlandish kind"
(Oswald, 63). The type belongs to the
family of *bâtarde* typefaces and antici-
pates the later subgroup of gothic
types called 'Schwabacher.'

Printing in France

31. Jacobus de Voragine
(ca. 1230–ca. 1298).
*Legenda aurea sanctorum, sive
Lombardica historia.*
Lyons: Mathias Huss, 20 July 1487.
Chancery F⁰.

Generally speaking, the early printed
vernacular editions of the *Legenda*

aurea had woodcut illustrations of the saints, while those in Latin did not. The exceptions to the latter rule are an edition printed by Günther Zainer in Augsburg, not after 1475 (Goff J–84), which reused the woodcuts of Zainer's German edition of 1471–72 (Goff J–156); and the two Lyons editions of Mathias Huss, 1486 and 1487, which used a newly commissioned series of 123 woodblocks. The completion date "20 July" in the colophon of this, the second of Huss's editions, is possibly inaccurate, for it may be blindly copied from the "20 July 1486" completion date in Huss's earlier edition. Huss used his woodcut series a third time, in his 17 December 1488 edition of the French version, *La legende doree*, which survives in only a single copy.

The Rutgers copy is one of about a dozen surviving; it formerly belonged to the Buenos Aires book collector Jorge Berestayn. Acquired by the Libraries through the Duncan Dunbar Sutphen Fund; 545524.

Reference: Goff J–118

32. Caesar, Julius. [*Works. 1519*] *Commentaria Caesaris nuperrime impressa: ab omnibus erratis accurate castigata…* Lugduni: Ex officina Guilhelmi Huyon, Anno M.D.XIX. Die autem XX. Decembris, leone X. Pont. Max. [i.e. 20 December 1519]. 8⁰.

Caesar's *Commentaria* was the first book to come from the press of Guillaume Huyon (fl. 1519–1520), of Lyon, in 1519. It is edited by Fra Giovanni Giocondo (ca. 1433–1515), an accomplished architectural engineer and author, with an index by Raimondo da Marliano.

The Rutgers copy is bound in early calf (rebacked) over wooden boards, stamped in blind, with gilt corner pieces, headbands, metal clasps (lacking), and blue upper edge; with early annotations; 360568.

Reference: BN v.25, col.875–876

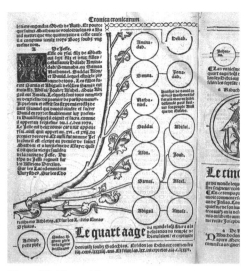

Entry 33, Figure 18.
Cronica cronicarum.
Paris: François Regnault and Jean Bonhomme,
1529. [1532?]
Actual size of page 20.5 x 15.5 cm.

Entry 34, Figure 19.
[Leaf 11] Book of Hours.
[Paris?: unknown, after 1500?]
Actual size of text block 20.5 x 12.5 cm.

58

33. *Cronica cronicarum abbrege et mis par figures, decentes et rondeaulx.*
Paris: François Regnault and Jean Bonhomme, '1529' [probably 1532].
4⁰.

François Regnault (d.1540) printed the *Cronica cronicarum*, a history of the world, in Paris, for Jean Bonhomme (d.1552), probably in 1532. Regnault came of a provincial family and began printing in about 1520. As is true of most printers, Regnault was more of a businessman than a fine printer or conscientious scholar. He is known chiefly for his successful relations with the English book trade, a specialty that demanded a fine degree of diplomacy and could at times prove hazardous. In 1538, while working on an English Bible, his printed sheets were seized and publicly burned, though Regnault escaped unharmed.

The *textura* titling type and *rotunda* text type used for the *Cronica cronicarum* suggest an older, more formal book aesthetic calculated to appeal to the merchants, physicians, and lawyers expected to buy it; their formality stands in vivid contrast with the book's robustly eclectic composition.

References: Adams C1495; *Éditions parisiennes* 1532.364

Loaned by Leonard Hansen, Class of '43

34. *[Leaf 7] [Book of Hours.* Paris?: unknown, after 1500?]

35. *[Leaf 8]* Schedel, Hartmann,
    (1440–1514).
    *[Liber chronicarum. German] Das Buch
    der Chroniken und Geschichten.*
    [Nuremberg: Anton Koberger, 1493].

    Woodcut map hand colored; two pages across "Der
    Werlt" Blat XIII. Schedel borrowed the world map
    from Ptolemy, without emending its obvious errors,
    or, more unfortunately, without including the news of
    Columbus's discoveries, which had recently been sent
    abroad. The border contains twelve dour windheads
    while the map is supported in three of its corners by
    the sober Old Testament figures of Shem, Japhet,
    and Ham.

36. *[Leaf 9]* Hortus Sanitatis.
    [Mainz: Jacob MaydenBach, 1471]

The following volumes in small formats, illustrated by
small woodcuts, reflect several significant cultural and
historical influences. Their petite size speaks to the spread
of reading and book ownership. Books like these could be
produced more cheaply than the grander-sized folio and
quarto volumes, and thus could be bought and used by
individuals of lesser means (enabling both a more diverse
audience and more specialized kinds of text). In addition,
the charming woodcuts here demonstrate the influence of
Geoffroy Tory (ca. 1480–ca. 1533), France's Imprimeur du
Roi, as well as a poet and gifted, if eccentric, typographical
designer. His *Champ Fleury* (1529) not only established the
use of the accent, apostrophe, and cedilla in French printing—without which written French would now be quite
changed—but it also popularized a kind of illustration in
which the thickness of the engraved lines balanced the
thickness of the lines in the letter forms. The equilibrium
of type and illustration enhanced the clarity of the illustrated page for which sixteenth century French printing
became renowned.

Entry 37, Figure 20
Biblia Sacra.
Paris: Pierre Regnault, 1541
Actual size of block 6.6 x 4.5 cm.

Even while France rose to become the center of printing in the West, civil violence and religious persecution worked to undermine her. After 1534, Catholic France grew progressively intolerant of Protestantism, and publishers who issued Protestant material faced considerable hazards: Étienne Dolet, who published Clément Marot's Calvinist satire *L'Enfer* (1542), met a gruesome death at the stake in Paris in 1546. With the subsequent death of François I, a year after Dolet's, the level of ferocity only intensified, and a large number of French printers were forced to flee to Geneva, including Henri and François Estienne, two of history's greatest scholar-printers (see #50). Publishers sympathetic to Protestant authors remaining in France therefore took care to protect their identities, such as omitting imprints from their publications—as we see in the works they published by Clément Marot and the zealous Calvinist Théodore de Bèze (1519–1605) (items #38–40).

37. *Biblia Sacra...* [v. II:]
Libri Regum – Iob. Paris:
Pierre Regnault, 1541.16⁰.

Geoffroy Tory's impact on French typography can be felt here, in the delicate woodcut. The penchant of French book design for decoration continued the French tradition of sumptuous manuscript illumination (see #28), which can also be observed in the illuminated border on the title mortice, and in the border of the French sixteenth-century *Book of Hours* (see #36, #A9).

Exhibition copy bound in early calf over pasteboard, with gilt and blind tooling on boards and spine, headbands, and gilt text edges; *provenance*: ex libris: Theodore Low De Vinne (1828–1914). De Vinne was one of the most admired of nineteenth-century American printers and printing historians. Stanley Morison called him "the greatest master-printer of his epoch" (Morison, *Letter Forms*, 71). Among his most valuable works on typography are his *The Practice of Typography* (1900–1904), *The Invention of Printing* (1876), and *Notable Printers of Italy During the Fifteenth Century* (1910).

Reference: Adams 1026

Loaned by Leonard Hansen, Class of '43

38. *Cinquante deux Pseaulmes de David. Traduictz en rithme francoyse selon la verite Hebraique, par Clément Marot.* [Lyons?: Jean Crespin?], 1546. 16°.

Son of the court poet Jean Marot (see #39), Clément far surpassed his father's accomplishments to become one of the finest poets of the French Renaissance. Literary historians trace the influence of his urbane wit in the poetry of his French contemporaries and, as well, the Elizabethans, in particular, Edmund Spencer (1552?–1599). Although the theologians of the Sorbonne condemned them, Marot's lyrical paraphrases of the psalms of David are now considered one of his principal claims to fame and mark the "beginning of modern French prosody" (Joseph, [1]). George Joseph attributes the source of the displeasure felt at the Sorbonne not to the quality of the paraphrases, but to Marot's having composed them in Geneva, the stronghold of Calvinism. Setting aside the hostility of the Sorbonne, the psalms have occasionally been criticized for nonpolitical reasons, too: Orentin Douen (1830–1896) reports that Voltaire scorned the elegant paraphrase of Psalm 68, *Que Dieu se montre seulement,* as fit to be sung by lecherous bodyguards (Douen, 1:471).

Entry 39, Figure 21.
Marot, Jean (1467?–1527?)
Recueil des oeuvres de Iehan Marot illustre poete francoys: Contenant. rondeaulx. epistres. vers espars. chantz royaulx.
[Lyon?: Denys d Harsy?], M.D.XXXV [1535]
Actual size of block 3.8 x 5.4 cm.

Marot, who had no Hebrew, is likely to have based his poems upon French and Latin translations made available to him.

Jean Crespin, the presumed printer, was born in Arras. In contrast to the many printers and punch-cutters who turned their talents as goldsmiths or calligraphers to the related tasks of casting or designing types, Crespin's career as a printer disjointedly followed upon a successful Parisian law practice, which religious persecution abbreviated. After embracing the reformed religion, in 1545 Crespin was compelled to flee Paris, ultimately landing in Geneva. On his flight he was accompanied by the scholar, Théodore de Bèze (#40), who later became the intimate of Jean Calvin (1509–1564). Turning printer in about 1551, Crespin published classical literature and books written in support of Calvinism. During his twenty-year career, he established a reputation both for the beauty and accuracy of his books and as a versatile man of letters.

The Rutgers copy is elegantly bound by the French binder Francisque Cuzin (1836–1890), in red morocco leather, with gilt tooling on boards, spine, board-edges and turn-ins; headbands with blue ribbon marker, marble endpapers and gauffered text edges; it was owned by Edouard Rahir (1862–1924), the French bibliophile, author, and art historian.

Reference: Johns (see *Bibliotheque d'Humanisme et Renaissance* (50, 1988, 87–93)

39. Marot, Jean (1467?–1527?)
Recueil des oeuvres de Iehan Marot illustre poete francoys:
Contenant. rondeaulx. epistres. vers espars. chantz royaulx.
[Lyon?: Denys d Harsy?], 1535. 16⁰.

Born in Normandy in about 1467, the poet Jean
Marot secured a position in the court of Anne
Bretagne, the wife of Louis XII, and, after her death,
remained to serve Francis I (then Duke Angoulême)
as *valet de chambre*. It is probable Marot served Louis as
scribe, secretary, and reader, as well (Joseph, [1]). Place
of publications and publisher unknown; attributions
based on Johns (see *Bibliotheque d'Humainisme et
Renaissance* (tome 1, 1988, p. 87-93).

40. Bèze, Théodore de.
Theodori Bezae Vezelii Poemata Iuvenilia.
[Paris?: unknown, after 1548]. 8⁰.

This copy of Bèze's poems is probably a second edition, issued in Paris shortly after the first edition of
1548. The title page, with its foreboding woodcut and
legend, *Maligna Loquuntur Super Me Mittentur In Inferi-
ora Terre* (Who speaks ill of me, may he be pitched into
hell), crackles with the religious conflicts of the age.
    With the lone exception of Jean Calvin, Théodore
de Bèze was sixteenth century Europe's most ardent
proponent of Calvinism, to which he converted upon
recovering from a debilitating illness. Predating his
conversion, however, his *Juvenilia*, a collection of
amorous verse, secured his reputation as a leading poet
of Latin.

The Rutgers copy is elegantly bound in red morocco
leather with French fillets tooled in gilt on boards,
gilt on spine, turn-ins, and board-edges, Dutch marble
endpapers, green ribbon marker, and gilt text edges;
provenance: Acquired by the Libraries through a fund
established by Robert H. Pruyn.

Entry 42, Figure 22.
[Amadìs de Gaula. French. 1541-1548]
Paris: Pour Vincent Sertenas, 1553.
Actual size of block 14.0 x 8.6 cm.

Reference: Frédéric Gardy, *Bibliographie des oeuvres… de Théodore de Bèze* (Geneva, 1960), nos. 2–3.

41. Burgo, Joannes de (d.1386).
Pupilla oculi omnibus presbyteris precipue Anglicanis summe necessaria.
Paris: Guillaume Hopyl for William Bretton and Henry Jacobi in London, 25 June 1510. F⁰.

Printed in Paris by Wolfgang Hopyl (d. 1522), edited by Augustin Agee. Wolfgang Hopyl came from The Hague or its environs and established himself in Paris by 1498. Although considered a technically skillful and artistic printer, Hopyl is more highly regarded for the accuracy of his compositors and the ability of his learned press correctors (see #15). His boast, that even if he were given a faulty manuscript, he could turn out a book almost without a flaw, was freely acknowledged by his contemporaries, both in Paris and abroad, who would send Hopyl books when they desired accurate, scholarly work. His example influenced the great scholar-printers of the sixteenth century. Along with his associate, Johann Higman (d. 1500), Hopyl specialized in books of philosophy, theology, and mathematics.

This copy is in an unrecorded sixteenth-century London binding of contemporary calf over wood, with brass clasps (missing), blind stamped with animal, bird, and floral designs

(rebacked). Bound in London for William Bretton,
a merchant, with whom Hopyl copublished several
other titles.

References: Adams B3303; *Éditions parisiennes* 1510.43;
STC 4115

Loaned by Leonard Hansen, Class of '43

42. [*Amadìs de Gaula. French.* 1541–1548] *Le Neufiesme
   Liure d'Amadis de gaule, auquel sont contenuz les gestes
   de dom Florisel de Niquée surnommé le chevalier de
   la Bergere...*
   Paris: Pour Vincent Sertenas, 1553. F⁰.

Most modern readers will be familiar with the *Amadìs
de Gaula* only through the mediation of Cervantes. In
his *Don Quixote,* Part One (Chapter VI), the priest and
barber survey Quixote's library, and it is the *Amadìs*
they first handle; later, in Part Two (Chapter I), the
priest gives pride of place to the *Amadìs* as "the first
book of chivalry printed in Spain." Indeed, despite its
relative obscurity in our century, scholars have called
the *Amadìs* one of the most influential works of prose
fiction ever published; by the end of the first quarter
of the seventeenth century it had been translated into
French, Italian, German, English, Dutch, Portuguese,
and Hebrew.

The first book of the French translation from the
original Spanish edition (1508) appeared in 1541 from
the press of Denis Janot (d. 1545), who published an
additional book every year until 1546 when the Sev-
enth Book appeared. An Eighth Book was added in
1548 and a Ninth in 1551, with subsequent books
issued randomly thereafter. For the beauty of their
illustrations, the first four books taken together have
been praised as one of the most remarkable illustrated
books published in Renaissance France.

The hero, Amadìs, a composite of Sir Lancelot and
Tristan, became for the French at once the idol of the
soldier, the courtier, and the poet; so warmly was he

received that a pious Jesuit, indignant at the licentiousness of this romance, disgustedly declared that the translation had been undertaken by the advice of Luther, under the immediate inspiration of the devil (Rose, p. viii–ix). More or less agreeing, the first English translator observed that the French version of the *Amadis* had, in fact, been made "more copious and wanton" (Thomas, 22).

The Rutgers copy is one of four volumes consisting of twelve books published 1541–1559; acquired for the Libraries through a library gift fund established by Charles H. Brower, '25, and Mrs. Brower.

Entry 43, Figure 23.
Vergilius Maro, Publius.
Opera Vergiliana docte & familiariter exposita.
Lyons: Jacques Sacon for Ciriaco Hochperg, 1517.
Actual size of block 18.3 x 13.8 cm.

43. Vergilius Maro, Publius.
Opera Vergiliana docte & familiariter exposita [with commentaries of Servius, Donatus, etc.].
Lyons: Jacques Sacon for Ciriaco Hochperg,
20 August–3 December 1517. F⁰.

Printed by Jacques Sacon (ca. 1472–1530), who printed at Lyons from about 1496 until 1530, this edition of Vergil's *Opera* is distinguished by its 214 woodcuts, consisting of 10 for the *Eclogues*, 39 for the *Georgics*, 143 for the *Aeneid*, and 21 for the miscellaneous poems at the end. These were originally printed in the 1502 Strassburg Vergil published by Johann Grüninger, apparently under the guidance of the great humanist scholar

Sebastian Brant (1458–1521), author of the *Narrenschiff* (#54). Grüninger, whose chief claim to fame lies in his publication of Martin Waldseemüller's *World Map* of 1507, the earliest surviving map to include the word *America*, is also known for having asserted that woodcuts make a book "a valuable thing" (Landau, 242). His inclination to privilege beauty over accuracy or utility typifies materialistic Strassburg at the time, an environment that proved conducive to the development of printmaking (see #12). The remarkably dense, allegorical designs in the *Works* characterize the rich narrative expressiveness of Italianate Classicism.

Reference: Baudrier XII, 344

44. *Biblia cum concordantijs Veteris & Noui Testamenti et sacrorum canonum.*
   Lyons: Jacques Sacon for Anton Koberger in Nuremberg,
   1 August 1512. F⁰.

Jaques Sacon of Lyons (see also #43) issued Anton Koburger's Vulgate Bible in several successive editions, beginning in 1511. While Albrecht Dürer's associate Hans Springinklee (1495?–1540?), created some of the illustrations, and Erhard Schön (d.1542?), another prominent Nuremburg artist, cut many of the illustrations for the Old Testament, many others were reengraved from various sources, including Bibles printed for

Entry 44, Figure 24.
Biblia cum concordantijs Veteris & Noui Testamenti et sacrorum canonum.
Lyons: Jacques Sacon for Anton Koberger in Nuremberg, 1512.
Actual size of block 21.8 x 16.6 cm.

Luca-Antonio Giunta (1457–1538), an important
Venetian printer and contemporary of Aldus
Manutius (#57).

Exhibition copy bound in contemporary blind
stamped vellum over wooden boards, with metal clasps
(missing); rebound with original vellum reattached;
once owned by the Benadictine monastery of
Ochsenhausen (1093–1803) in Württemberg.

Reference: Adams B988; Baudrier XII, 330
Loaned by Leonard Hansen, Class of '43

Gallery '50
Printing in England

E ngland's first printer was native born, a boast that no
other European country but Germany could make.
Born in the Weald of Kent, William Caxton (ca. 1422–
1491) first prospered as a cloth merchant in Bruges, where
he attained the prestigious position of "governor" of all
English merchants, and served as an English diplomat.
When Caxton opened his printing office in Bruges, it was
not for the usual purpose of fashioning a livelihood, but in
order to self-publish his English translation of Raoul
Lefèvre's *Recueil des histoires de Troye*, which he undertook
at the pleasure of Margaret, Duchess of Burgundy. Caxton
and his partner, Colard Mansion, a calligrapher attached to
the Burgundian court, published the *Recueil* between 1474
and 1476, making it the first printed book to appear in the
English language. Upon returning alone to England in
1476, Caxton established the first press on English soil, in
the abbey precincts at Westminster. (Printing historians cite
this typographical beachhead as the possible source for the
colloquialism, 'a chapel of printers,' to refer to the printers
within a particular shop.) Of the 100+ books Caxton
published, more than half were in English, including the
editio princeps of several of the immortal works of early
English poetry, including Geoffrey Chaucer's *Canterbury
Tales* (1478), John Gower's *Confessio Amantis* (1483), and
Thomas Malory's *Le Morte d'Arthur* (1485).

At the time Caxton opened his first print shop, Bruges
was a rich, cosmopolitan city, renowned for its production
of expensive, deluxe manuscripts. Although his original
typeface comes directly from Mansion, and indirectly
from the Flemish *bâtarde* manuscripts Mansion imitated,
Caxton's later types reflect the influence of early fifteenth-
century English manuscripts.

Caxton's assistant, Wynkyn de Worde (d. 1534), succeeded him after his death, becoming, in 1491, England's
second printer and its most prolific. Worde published 800
works, many of which were school books, his specialty.

The type in Worde's *Dives and Pauper* is a condensed *textura*, which Alfred Forbes Johnson calls one of the "best productions of that generation" (151). In 1528, Worde became the first English printer to employ an italic face (see also #49), importing it from The Netherlands.

45. *Dives and Pauper.*
London: Wynkyn de Worde,
3 December 1496. Chancery F[0].

Second edition, reprinted from Richard Pynson's first edition of 5 July 1493 (Goff P–117). Incunable catalogs continue to attribute the Middle English devotional tract *Dives and Pauper* (Rich Man and Poor Man), a dialogue structured on the Ten Commandments, to one Henry Parker, a Carmelite who flourished in the 1460s. In fact it has long been established that the still-anonymous *Dives and Pauper* was written long before Parker was born—probably between about 1405 and 1410, as it contains references to specific events in England during those years. Pynson's edition, for which the manuscript printer's copy is preserved in the Bodleian Library, was nonillustrated. Wynkyn's reprint added three woodcuts, two from his existing stock, and one, representing the disputants *Dives and Pauper*, which was made for the edition. A third and last edition in octavo format was printed in 1536.

Entry 45, Figure 25.
Dives and Pauper.
London: Wynken de Worde, 1496.
Actual size of block 18.0 x 11.3 cm.

The Rutgers copy was formerly in the collection of Sir Henry Mildmay, Bart., with the Dogmersfield Library bookplate.

Reference: Goff P-118

46. *Chronicles of England* and *Description of Britain*. London: Wynkyn de Worde, May 1502. Chancery F⁰.

Wynkyn de Worde's second edition. The *Chronicles of England*, based on the fourteenth-century French *Brut d'Angleterre* with continuations going to the year 1461, were first published by William Caxton in 1480. He produced the *Description of England*, an extract from the English version of Ranulph Higden's *Polycronicon*, several months later as a topographic supplement. In about 1485 the still-mysterious schoolmaster-printer in Saint Albans produced an enlarged version of the *Chronicles*, with a prefatory chapter starting with Adam and Eve, and supplementary chronicles and events going into the 1470s. In 1497 Wynkyn de Worde reprinted this Saint Albans version, which from that point onward replaced Caxton's version. Seven more editions of the Saint Albans *Chronicles* appeared through 1528. In the words of the historian Antonia Gransden, the *Brut Chronicles* thus "reached the Tudors, to be plundered by the historians Edward Hall and Raphael Holinshed and through them to provide Shakespeare with copy." (*–pn*)

The Rutgers copy bound in diced Russia, with marble text edges, gilt spine, marbled endpapers; *provenance*: ex libris Marquises of buton, with Luton Library bookplate; acquired for the Libraries through the Curlett N. Wilhelm Book Fund; 733524.

Reference: STC 9997

47. Gower, John (1325?–1408).
De Confessione amantis.
London: Thomas Berthelet, 13 March 1554. F⁰.

This, the third edition of Gower's *Confessio amantis,*
was printed in London by Thomas Berthelet in 1554;
originally published by William Caxton in 1483.
Berthelet, who reprinted Caxton's *Confessio Amantis,*
began publishing in about 1525, eventually replacing
Worde's frequent collaborator, Richard Pynson, as the
King's printer.

The Rutgers copy bound in panel-stamped calf with
gilt on board edges; it was acquired for the Libraries
through a library gift fund established by Charles H.
Brower, '25, and Mrs. Brower; 733181.

Reference: STC 12144

Scholar-Printers

Aldo Manuzio—better known by the Latinized form
of his name, Aldus Manutius (1449 or 1450–1515)—
was the first great scholar-printer, whose engagement with
classical learning, close contact with learned communities,
and forceful business practices enabled him to bring into
print the unpublished cornerstone texts of Greek and
Roman literature—particularly Greek philosophy. Aldus
published the *editio princeps* of Hesiod (1495), Aristotle
(1495–1498), Aristophanes (1498), Sophocles (1502), Plato
(1513), and more than twenty other seminal authors of
antiquity. As Barbara A. Shailor has noted in this catalog,
if Aldus had not secured these texts in print, their survival
beyond the manuscript era would have been uncertain, and
Western literature would have lost some of its earliest
guiding lights.

Aldus figures prominently in the history of type design
as well. In collaboration with the ingenious goldsmith
and punch-cutter, Francesco Griffo of Bologna, he created
typefaces that largely determined the appearance of

sixteenth-century scholarly publication. His Roman, designed in 1495, modernized Jenson's prototypical Roman (see #16). By reducing the size of Jenson's epigraphic capitals, he brought them into greater harmony with the minuscules. (Bembo, the typeface of this catalog, is an early twentieth-century imitation of Aldus's Roman, and named after Cardinal Pietro Bembo (1470–1547), the author of the original fifteenth-century text in which it appeared). Aldus's four Greek fonts, produced between 1495 and 1502, modeled upon the contemporary freeflowing handwriting of Immanuel Rhusotas rather than the ancient more formal hand beloved by early humanists, are both praised as technologically innovative (Barker, 11), and criticized for "want of legibility" (Davis, 14), for their excessive use of ligatures. Finally the type designed by Griffo upon the 'cancelleresca corsiva' of the Papal Chancery (probably the hand of Bartolomeo Sanvito), first printed as the face of a complete text in the Aldine Vergil of (April) 1501, marks the entrance into the world of what we know familiarly as italic. Highly regarded in appearance—Erasmus esteemed italic to be "the neatest types in the world," and economical—its slanting lines allowed more letters to appear per page, and therefore required less paper, italic became almost as popular as Roman during the sixteenth century. As exhibited here (see items #32, 49, 50, 51), the texts of small, scholarly publications of the sixteenth century or, rather, classical texts for the nonscholarly ideal reader, who had the education and leisure to read classical literature, but whose reading matter was not wholly dictated by his profession—appeared completely in italic, a practice that may seem strange to those of us who are accustomed to seeing italic used for emphasis or to set off words in a foreign language.

Entry 48, Figure 26.
Urbanus Bellunensis (Urbano 1442–1524).
Institutiones Graecae grammatices.
Venice: Aldus Manutius, 1497.
Actual size of page 13.2 x 10.2 cm.

48. Urbanus Bellunensis
(Urbano 1442–1524).
Institutiones Graecae grammatices.
Venice: Aldus Manutius, January 1497.
Super-Chancery 4⁰.

The first of several great accomplishments of the scholar-printer Aldus Manutius (ca. 1450–1515) was to inaugurate, from 1494 onward, a comprehensive program of Greek publishing. This comprehended not just his multivolume Aristotle (1495–1498) and other major classical texts, but also various smaller helps to studying Greek. In 1495 he had printed the grammars of two native Greeks, Theodore Gaza and Constantine Lascaris, but neither was suited for non-native beginners. Aldus commissioned, therefore, the present grammar, written in Latin. Incunable catalogs generally date the work to January 1498, assuming that its colophon, "M.IIID. mense Ianuario," followed the Venetian custom of year-changes at 1 March rather than the 1 January of the Roman year. This interpretation is doubtful, however. In the Greek dictionary *Thesaurus Cornucopiae*, completed by Aldus in August 1496, he stated that Urbano's grammar was shortly to appear.

The author, Fra Urbano of Belluno, was a Franciscan monk who had earlier traveled extensively in the Levant and in the 1480s had been in Florence, where he tutored Giovanni de' Medici (future pope Leo X). In the 1490s he resettled in the convent dei Frari in Venice, and gained a considerable reputation there as a teacher of

Greek. Aldus dedicated Urbano's grammar to
Gianfrancesco Pico della Mirandola (1469–1533),
nephew of the philosopher Giovanni Pico, count of
Mirandola (1463–1494), who had been a close friend
and patron of Aldus's. In 1512 Urbano produced an
enlarged and heavily revised edition, which was
frequently reprinted into the 1560s.

The early editions identify Urbanus simply by his
Christian name (which is how Aldus identified him),
or as Urbanus Bellunensis—of Belluno—or as
Urbanus Bolzanius. His true family name appears
to have been Dalle Fosse. Several recent studies have
misnamed him Urbano Valeriano, but this is an
invented surname taken on for its ancient connota-
tions by his nephew, the humanist Piero Valeriani
(1477–1558); Urbano did not use it.

Reference: Goff U–66

49. Sallust (86–34 B.C.)
De conivratione Catilinae …De bello Iugurthino [and
other works] Venice: Aldus Manutius, April 1509. 8^0.

Printed in Venice by Aldus Manutius, in 1509, this edition of Sallust is one of Aldus's so-called "handbooks"
(*enchiridia*)—small classical texts, bearing his anchor
and dolphin (a graphic restatement of the motto,
festina lente, "make haste slowly"), of which Erasmus
said memorably, the image is known wherever good
learning is cherished.

The Rutgers copy bound in early calf binding
stamped blind and in gold, with gauffered text edges.

Reference: Adams S139; Renouard Alde 57(3)

Entry 50, Figure 27.
Cato, Marcus Porcius, 234–149 B.C.
Libri de re rustica: M. Cantonis Lib. 1.
Paris: Robert Estienne, 1543.
Actual size of block 5.4 x 4.0 cm.

Entry 51, Figure 28.
Trissino, Giovanni Giorgio (1478–1550).
La poetica di M. Gio Van Giorgio Trissino.
Vicenza: Tolomeo Ianiculo, 1529.
Actual size of text block 16 x 9.9 cm.

50. Cato, Marcus Porcius (234–149 B.C.).
Libri de re rustica: M. Catonis Lib. I: M. Terrentii Varronis Lib. III
[ed. Pietro Vettori]. Paris: Robert Estienne, 17 July 1543. 8⁰.

Printed in Paris by Robert Estienne (1503?–1559) in 1543. Robert and his son, Henri II (1531–98), are the two preeminent scholar-printers of their century (Steinberg, 86). No less revered than Aldus's anchor and dolphin device, the Estienne olive tree, with its biblical inscription, *noli altum sapere, sed timet* (be not high-minded, but fear) urges wonder, humility, and devotion, suggesting that greater learning reveals with equal clarity the overawing majesty of the Creator, the *mysterium tremendum,* and the true insignificance of a man. Like many of the classical texts of its time, Estienne's *De agricultura* appears completely in italic.

The Rutgers copy bound in limp vellum, bearing ink stamps from Hoxton Academy and Highbury College; acquired for the Libraries with Federal Funds; 213805.

Reference: Adams S817

51. Trissino, Giovanni Giorgio (1478–1550).
La poetica di M. Gio Van Giorgio Trissino.
Vicenza: Tolomeo Ianiculo, April 1529. 4⁰.

Trissino's poetry, together with his epistolary writings on the Italian language and his translation of

Dante's *De vulgari eloquentia* (the *editio princeps* of this important work), comprise the *Opere*, printed by Tolommeo Janicolo (fl. 1524–1548), in 1529, in the graceful italic of the calligrapher, Ludovico degli Arrighi. Janicolo, or perhaps Trissino, purchased it from Arrighi sometime after 1525. A Roman writing-master of exceptional gifts, Arrighi modified the cursive letters used in the Papal Chancery in a publication he designed to teach calligraphy to laymen. These were in turn cut by the goldsmith, Lautizio Perugino (fl. 1524–1525). Their delicacy and quirky expressiveness (note the interpolation of the Greek omega, into a Latin alphabet) exercised a strong influence on the subsequent development of italic type, both in Italy and abroad, and survives in slightly modified form in the fine printing of our own time.

Reference: Adams T955

Printing's Spread Beyond the Mainstream

Spain

52. [Albert, Miguel, ed.]
    Repertorium de pravitate haereticorum.
    Valencia: [Miguel Albert], 16 September 1494.
    Chancery F⁰.

The "Repertory on the Depravity of Heretics" was an official reference work of the Office of the Inquisition in Spain, an alphabetical dictionary of legal topics for the guidance of inquisitors. Like most medieval law books, both manuscript and printed, the text is highly abbreviated, and thus aimed at users who had formal training in civil and canon law. The colophon names Miguel Albert of Valencia, doctor of both laws, as the editor. Records in the archives of Valencia show that Dr. Albert contracted with an official of the Inquisition in Valencia, Juan Gómez de Çarrion, to share the costs of producing an edition of 1,000 copies of the *Repertorium*: Gómez to provide the paper, and Albert to provide the types and labor. (It may be noted that the paper, locally made, is of highest quality.) Albert was involved in the production of at least five other Valencian incunables, some in Latin and some in Catalan.

Reference: Goff R–148

Low Countries

53. [Cato: Disticha Catonis].
Moralissimus Cato cum elegantissimo commento
(by Robertus de Euromodio).
Antwerp: Gerard Leeu, 30 October 1487.
Chancery 4⁰.

About 150 surviving incunable editions were printed of the late classical maxims commonly called *Cato* or *Disticha Catonis*: a collection of hexameter couplets to which the name of the famously upright Roman citizen Cato the Censor was attached. The incunable printings represent a wide range of versions, with or without various commentaries and supplementary texts, and in various translations, both prose and verse, into Dutch, English, French, Low and High German, Italian, and Spanish. So many of these editions survive in only a single copy that it is likely that others have disappeared entirely. The chief audience for all these editions was the young, *adolescentes*, whether for formal school reading and memorization, or for less formal vernacular instruction.

This edition is the last of three published by Gerard Leeu in Antwerp (1485, 1486, 1487), all of which display a striking title woodcut of a master and pupil, recycled by Leeu from a Dutch devotional text published by him in 1484. Leeu's editions add a commentary composed by a Cistercian of Clairvaux, Robert of Evremond (d. 1480), addressed by him to a pupil, one Pietro of Saluzzo. The commentary first appeared, in

slightly different form, in a Constance edition of
ca. 1473. Leeu's version became popular, and was
reprinted by other European shops in thirteen more
incunable editions, some of which copied his distinctive title-page cut. The Rutgers copy of the
1487 edition is one of five recorded, and the only in
this country.

The Distichs of Cato continued in popularity long
after 1500. There were influential editions by Erasmus
and by Joseph Scaliger among others. An English
translation made for his daughters by James Logan of
Philadelphia was printed by Benjamin Franklin, 1735,
the first classical work to be printed in America.

Reference: Goff C–299a

54. Turrecremata, Johannes de (ca. 1388–1468).
Tractatus de venerabili sacramento de corpore Christi.
Delft: Jacob Janszoon van der Meer,
[ca. 1481–1482]. Chancery 4⁰.

Card. Juan de Torquemada (Turrecremata), uncle of
the infamous Spanish inquisitor, was, with his friend
Nicholas of Cusa, one of the two chief defenders of
papal authority in his century. Like Cusa, it is known
that Torquemada was an early enthusiast for the new
invention of typography. (In *De Idiota* (1450) Cusa's
remarkable notion of a continuously expanding library
seems to anticipate and extend spiritual authority to
the development of movable type—*mj*.) He was, in
fact, apparently the first author to commission a
printed edition of one of his own writings. Torquemada's *Meditationes* on the frescoes of Santa Maria
sopra Minerva in Rome, the church where he would
be buried, were printed in Rome by Ulrich Han, with
woodcuts based on the frescoes, in an edition dated
31 December 1467 (perhaps to be interpreted as
1466), the first woodcut-illustrated book printed in
Italy and possibly the first book printed in Rome.
More than sixty incunable editions of various of

Torquemada's spiritual and doctrinal writings are known. This Delft book, with the fine woodcut device of the first printer of that city, Jacob van der Meer, is the only incunable edition of Torquemada's treatise on the Eucharist, composed by him in Basel, 1436. At least two sixteenth-century editions are known.

The Rutgers copy bound in quarter leather: formerly owned by George Dunn, with pencil notations on front cover and fly-leaf; acquired by the Libraries through a fund established by Charles H. Brower '25 and Mrs. Brower; 665806 (–*mj*).

Reference: Goff T–557

55. Crescentiis, Petrus de (ca. 1233–ca. 1320).
     Ruralia commoda.
     Louvain: Johannes de Westfalia,
     9 December 1474. Chancery F⁰.

FIRST EDITION. The first fully dated book printed in Louvain, the sole university town of the Low Countries. Johannes de Westfalia had earlier printed in Alost (1473–1474), in partnership with Thierry Martens, using the same type font as in his first Louvain edition. Johannes de Westfalia's colophon describes the font as a "littera vera modernata, abscisa, et formata," a phrase difficult to translate with precision, but apparently referring in part to its clarity of design. The punches for the font were almost certainly cut in Venice, and it is likely that both Johannes de Westfalia and Thierry Martens had learned the printing trade there. Johannes de Westfalia remained the dominant printer of Louvain to the end of the century. He marketed his books vigorously in England as well as locally.

The *Ruralia commoda* of Crescenzi or Crescentiis is the most important medieval treatise on agronomy, and continues to be studied for its diverse information on many aspects of medieval rural life. Its author was a well-off Bolognese advocate and member of the city's

senate. He composed his treatise at about the age of
seventy, when he retired from the city to his country
estate, Villa dell'Olmo; he states that he wrote at the
request of his friend Aimerico da Piacenza, General
of the Dominican order. The *Ruralia commoda* maintained its reputation as a practical encyclopedia for
about three hundred years. Besides its manuscript
tradition, it became frequently printed in the original
Latin, and in Italian, French, and German versions.
There were even two Polish-language editions
(1549, 1571).

Reference: Goff C–966

Some Rarities in the Collection

56. Platina, Bartholomaeus (1421–1481).
    De honesta voluptate et valetudine.
    Cividale: Gerardus de Lisa, 24 October 1480.
    Chancery 4^0.

The first book printed in Cividale, 115 km northeast
of Venice. Its printer, Gerardus de Lisa, was Flemish.
The path that brought him to Italy and into the printing trade is unknown. He was the first printer of Treviso (1471), and after producing about twenty editions
there he wandered, emerging as printer successively in
Venice (1477–1478), in Treviso again (1478), in Cividale (1480), in neighboring Udine (1484–1485), and
then for a third time in Treviso (1492–1494). Little
further is known of his biography other than that he
married a native of Udine, and that by 1500 she was
a widow.

Platina's *De honesta voluptate*, which first appeared in
a Venice edition of 1475, is the earliest printed cook-
ery book. Platina, a versatile humanist, also composed
a much-reprinted history of the lives of the popes, and
in 1475 was named by Sixtus IV as librarian of the
Vatican. His *De honesta voluptate*, which besides recipes

proper contains many prescriptions for health, was printed in some eighteen Latin editions through 1540, as well as in several vernacular versions. De Lisa's edition, though printed—at his own costs, he records—in an obscure town, was clearly widely distributed, suggesting that a major part of the edition was sent to Venice. About seventy-five copies still survive today. After De Lisa's printing shop closed down in late 1480, no further printing is known from Cividale until the later eighteenth century.

Reference: Goff P–763

57. Fliscus, Stephanus (fl. 1424–1462).
     Sententiarum variationes.
     (Latin-French; with other texts). [Paris: Philippe Pigouchet, after 1491]. Chancery 4^0.

Stephanus Fliscus is, so far as his tradition in print is concerned, a man of one book, but that book was quite popular in its age. He was a native of Soncino, but widely traveled. In the 1420s he was in Normandy as secretary to the Italian bishop of Lisieux, and for fifteen years, 1444 to 1459, was schoolmaster in Ragusa, from where he went to Venice in 1460 as schoolmaster of Santa Marina. His *Sententiarum variationes*, or *Synonyma*, apparently compiled in 1437, is a school text for Latin prose composition, providing a series of variant ways of expressing oneself in Latin. Thus, for "God help us," one may write "Deus nos adiuvet," "Deus sit nobis propitius," "Deus sit nobis in adiutorio," etc. More than three dozen incunable editions survive, with the leading phrases printed in various vernaculars according to the regions where the editions were sold: Dutch, French, German, Low German, French, and Spanish. Pigouchet's edition is apparently the third with French captions, preceded by a Turin edition of 1481 (uniquely preserved at the Pierpont Morgan Library), and a Lyons edition of the later 1480s. These editions supplemented Fliscus's *Synonyma* with the tract *De eloquentia* of Gasparinus Barzizius, and a late

classical *Synonyma*, falsely ascribed to Cicero. Fliscus's
Synonyma continued to be reprinted into the early
sixteenth century, but then was dealt its death blow
by the appearance of Erasmus's greatly superior
Copia (1512).

The Rutgers copy is one of three recorded, the others
being at the Bibliothèque Nationale de France, Paris,
and Trinity College, Dublin.

Reference: GW 10015 (not in Goff)

58. *[Print 4]* Bloemaert, Abraham (1564–1651).
    The Magdalen reading.
    Mid-seventeenth century. Engraving.

    Loaned by the Jane Voorhees Zimmerli Art Museum,
    Rutgers, The State University of New Jersey
    Gift of Dr. M. Roy Fisher.

59. *[Leaf 10]* Bible. German. 1483.
    [Nuremburg: Anton Koberger, 1483]
    Hand-colored woodcut illustration of Abraham and
    the Three Angels (see also #30).

    Loaned by the Jane Voorhees Zimmerli Art Museum,
    Rutgers, The State University of New Jersey

Art Library
Illustration

The ten illustrations exhibited here demonstrate a variety of illustrative approaches and engraving methods favored by the first artists and artisans of the printed book. It is difficult to generalize too broadly about illustration during the period under consideration, as it was an era of rapid innovation and varied production. One can however note that scholarly study of the earliest illustrated books focuses on several interrelated characteristics. Early woodcuts tend to be simple in design, meant to achieve maximum legibility and swift "readability" of the image; the image sometimes symbolizes, rather than iterates or hypostatizes, a specific textual element. Contrary to modern practices, a woodcut might be printed multiple times within a text and represent two or more different cities or personages (as in Schedel's *Liber chronicarum*—#A1), different saints or martyrs (as in the *Legenda Aurea*—#31), or different scenes in an imaginary narrative (as in Dante's *La Commedia*—#18). While a modern audience might find this nonrepresentational approach to illustration inadequate or disconcerting, Renaissance readers understood that illustrations gestured toward realities underlying the particulars of the text, and lent historically separate events a degree of relationship, constructive coherence, and intelligibility. Perhaps they also accepted that the expense and beauty of a woodcut justified its redundancy.

A1. *[Leaf 11]* Schedel, Hartmann (1440–1514).
[Liber chronicarum]. Liber cronicarum.
Nuremberg: Anton Koberger, 1493.

German book illustration profited from a highly organized relationship between publisher and artist. Hartmann Schedel's *liber chronicarum,* or *Weltchronik,* serves as a prime example. Painter Michel Wolgemut and Wilhelm Pleydenwurff cut 645 wood blocks to form a suite of over 1,800 illustrations in the final text. Many views of town and cityscapes are included, though Arthur Hind notes that there exists "only a beginning of a faithful topography in the views" (Hind, 375). Certainly, faithfulness could not decently be claimed when a woodcut illustrating Maguncia (i.e., Mainz, the birthplace of printing), also must illustrate Lyon, Bologna, Naples, and several other European cities as well. As Dale Roylance notes, such duplication remained acceptable in a period hovering between the late Gothic and early Renaissance due to "a lingering medieval regard for symbol over reality" [i.e., material actuality] (Roylance, 14). (See also #4.)

A2. *[Leaf 12] Bible. German. 1483.*
[Nuremburg: Anton Koberger, 1483]
Hand-colored woodcut illustration from the Book of Exodus (see #30).

The effective simplicity of early German book illustration is evidenced in a leaf from the German Bible *(Bible. German. 1483)* of Anton Koberger. In a scene from Exodus (7. 8 10), Moses and Aaron are sent by God to deliver the Israelites from Egypt. As Aaron throws down his staff in front of the pharaoh, it immediately becomes a serpent. In the accompanying illustration, the primary characters, Pharaoh, Aaron, and Moses, are positioned frieze-like across the picture plane, and are identified by label. Despite the elaborate architectural backdrop, the scene is minimally landscaped, drawing attention to the human participants and the radically transforming staff. "Vivid hand-ground colors so characteristic of the fifteenth century" serve to set the woodcut starkly apart from the surrounding text (Roylance, 12).

A3. *[Leaf 13]* Brant, Sebastian (1458–1521).
[Das Narrenschiff. Latin]
Strassburg: Johann Grüninger, 1 June 1497.

Wolgemut's most famous pupil, Albrecht Dürer, reached his artistic maturity with works such as the artist's sixteenth-century masterpiece, *The Apocalypse*. The woodcut illustrations for Sebastian Brant's *Narrenschiff*, or *Ship of Fools* (see also #43), represent the earlier, more emphatically Gothic flavor of his work, executed before his trip to Italy and its concomitant classicizing influences (Hind, 381). Although there remains some doubt about the attribution of all of the *Narrenschiff*'s woodcuts to Dürer, the illustration exhibited here demonstrates the strengths of Dürer's early work. As one helpless fool is being trampled by a horse, the second fool looks indifferently into the distance. He too is in precarious proximity to the horse's bucking hind legs. Yet his obliviousness is signaled by his dulled expression and protruding tongue. Dürer succeeds in focusing the viewer's attention on the intricacies of the foreground trio, while the craggy landscape recedes into the background.

Loaned by Leonard Hansen, Class of '43

Entry A3, Figure 29.
[Leaf 14] Brant, Sebastian (1458–1521).
[Das Narrenschiff. Latin]
Strassburg: Johann Grüninger, 1 June 1497.
Actual size of block 11.5 x 8.5 cm.

A4. Thuróczy, János (b. ca. 1435).
Der Hungern Chronica inhlatend wie sie anfenkglich ins
land kommen sind mit anzeygung irem aller irer König
Athila un[d] volfüuret biss auff König Ludwig so im 1526.
Jar bey Mohatz vom Türcken umbkomen ist.
In Wien: in Druck verordnet auss Kosten und
Darlegen Hansen Metzkers, anno domini 1534. F⁰.

Illustrations in various styles, signed "PF."

Peter Flötner (1485–1546) was a Nuremburg sculptor
who also made prints and probably cut the blocks
himself. His *Veit Bildhauer*, "*Veit* the sculptor," affords
us an interesting glimpse of the tensions between
creativity and commerce in his cut of an artist turned
mercenary. "An unrecorded state of this print carries a
short verse text in which a lansquenet laments how he
once carved beautiful images, 'artistic in both the Italian and the German fashion,' but that no one any
longer values these. Therefore, though he could cut
naked figures which would easily sell 'in Mark and
Stetten,' this is not to his taste, and he has thus been
driven to take up his halberd and go off to serve a
prince" (Landau, 214).

Exhibition copy bound in marbled paper over boards;
paper lettering piece on spine; *provenance*: bears the
ex libris of Prince Lichtenstein.

Loaned by Leonard Hansen, Class of '43

A5. [*Leaf 14*] Unidentified. [German? about 1500?]

Six lines of German verse in a large Gothic *bâtarde*,
with a large Italianate woodcut, hand-colored.

Loaned by Leonard Hansen, Class of '43

A6. *[Bible, Latin]. Biblia cum concordantijs veteris et noui testa-menti & sacrorum canonum.* Venice: Lucantonio Giunta, 28 May 1511.

The Rutgers copy bound in eighteenth-century calf; unidentified arms in gilt on both covers, a chevron between three trefoils; *provenance:* formerly owned by the eminent bibliophile and author C.W. Dyson Perrins (1864–1958), with his ex libris.

Reference: Adams B987

A7. Pliny the Elder. *Historia naturale di Caio Plinio Secondo: di lingua latina in fiorentina tradocta per il doctissimo homo misser Christophero Landino fiorentino.* Venice: Melchiorre Sessa & Pietro di Ravani compagni [ca. 1516?]

A8. Vergilius Maro, Publius. *[Aeneid, Italian:] Virgilio volgare qual narra le aspre battaglie & li fatti di Enea nuovamente historiato.* Venice: Niccolò Zoppino, 1528.

Alfred Pollard has commented upon the "delicacy of touch" evident in Venetian woodcuts (Pollard, *Book Illustration,* 209). In the illustrations for Vergil's *Aeneid* (#59), the fall of Troy is clearly represented by Aeneas standing next to the Trojan horse, while a small-scale city burns in the distant background. The evident components—the city, the horse, and Aeneas—seem entirely self-contained and self-sufficient. What Eleanor Leach has observed about an early English edition of the *Aeneid* holds here. "Aeneas seldom appears within the confines of these cities but stands, rather, outside their walls…. His exclusion, as it were, from walls, which so often serve as the symbol of his longing for a fixed home, quite effectively conveys the sense of restless exile that pervades the narrative" (Leach, 191). Again, the content of the independent illustration is couched within broader cultural narratives.

A9. *[Leaf 15]* [*Book of Hours.* Paris?: unknown, after 1500]

The early book illustration of France was largely
determined by the French manuscript tradition. Books
of Hours replete with decorated woodcut borders
originated in France in the last decades of the fifteenth
century. The leaf displayed here is composed of a complex six-part decorative border. Beneath a shepherd
watching his flock is a finely detailed scene of the
Adoration of the Shepherds. In a scene pitched from
foreground to background, Mary sits holding the
infant Christ, who benevolently extends his left arm
to the group. The Magi, in exotic costume, are joined
in their worship by an equal number of shepherds.
The shepherd in the left foreground has cast aside his
hat and staff. He raises his arms, while holding his
musical instrument, in gesture of both offering and
astonishment. Symbolizing the coincidence of the
prosaic and the profound, and serving as evidence of
the engraver's inordinate ability to realize fine detail in
the difficult medium of a small woodcut, a tiny dog
curls up in the center foreground.

Loaned by Leonard Hansen, Class of '43

A10. Marot, Clément (1495?–1544). *L'adolescence Clémen-
tine· Aultrément. Les oeuvres de Clément Marot, valet de
chambre du Roy, faictes en son adolesce[n]ce. Avec le residu
despuys faict. Le tout selon sa derniere recognoissance.*
[Paris?: s.n.], M.D.XXXIIII [1534]

Reference: Cf *Editions parisiennes* lists 2 1534 Paris editions:
(a) 1534.1069: Paris: Louis Blaubloom veuve de Pierre
Roffet, 7 March 1534. 8% —(b) 1534.1070: Paris: Louis
Blaubloom veuve de Pierre Roffet, 19 August 1534. 8%.
Rutgers copy lacks imprint statement of these items, and
may be unique.

Rare Times with Rare Books

by Leonard Hansen,

Class of '43

It was in my senior year at Rutgers, 1942, that I took a noncredit Team Teaching course on the history of the arts in Western Civilization. The course, taught by Howard McKinney (music), Donald Cameron (literature), and Franklin Biebel (art and architecture), met late on Monday afternoons. This meant I would arrive tardy for football practice. It was understood that an essential "lab" course was the cause. One can imagine the shock and disbelief when the assistant coach investigated and found that the history of art took precedence over football.

This was my first exposure to the visual arts. After four years in the infantry, marriage, three children, and a small real estate business, my wife Eleanor and I began to collect antiques and European works of art. We refinanced our home in Englewood, NJ, in 1960 and took time off to spend five days at the Plaza Hotel in New York City. We planned to enjoy the museums, the theater, and restaurants. To my complete surprise we spent the entire money on four early works of art. Returning home overwhelmed, I knew that while Eleanor had the good taste and eye to distinguish an authentic piece from a false one, I would have to further educate myself. I began systematically to take courses in art history at the New School, the Metropolitan Museum of Art, and the Institute of Fine Arts in New York City. My education focused on medieval and Renaissance studies.

In 1969 I took a course at the Institute under Professor Colin Eisler, on the History of Prints from the mid-fifteenth century to the advent of photography. It was there that I discovered the book as a work of art and learned to more knowledgeably enjoy its extraordinary handmade paper, the precise bite of the print, the woodcut, the sumptuous engravings, and one-of-a-kind decorative binding. I now saw the early printed book as an exquisitely beautiful artwork that also contained a rich world of learning within its pages. Furthermore, at a time when the price of art and antiques began to skyrocket, early printed books were still reasonable. I was hooked. For the next twenty-five years I was passionately involved in acquiring books and manuscripts. I constantly attended auctions in New York and purchased from rare book dealers all over the United States and Europe.

My early collecting included books in several languages, but I gradually settled on British books, with an emphasis on the Tudor and Stuart periods, as well as single pages of illuminated manuscripts. When my four sons moved out of my home, it was amazing how quickly their rooms were transformed into libraries. It also meant I had to develop my own reference library in order to throughly research my early books.

My life has been immensely enriched by books. Twenty-five years ago, I acquired a copy of the Great Bible from a New York dealer. During a visit to St. John's College Library in Cambridge, England, I was with a group of scholars and we came upon the magnificent illuminated presentation copy of the first edition of the Great Bible (1539) given to Henry VIII. This was the same book I owned, albeit mine was a much-used copy, made up of several of the seven editions. This was not unusual because Henry VIII had issued a proclamation that one copy be chained to every Cathedral and parish church throughout the British Isles. As the librarian turned the pages, I realized that my copy in its much-used condition was an important book.

About twelve years ago I met the then director of the Bodleian Library of Oxford, David Vaisey, at the Grolier Club in New York City. I mentioned to him that I had a splendid two-volume edition, in Latin, of the works of Cicero. The volumes were published in Paris in 1550 and bore an inscription on the flyleaf written in both Latin and in Greek to John Lawther, a member of the British Parliament. It was signed, Thomas Barlow, who was the third director of the Bodleian Library (1642–1660).

The following year, while touring England and Wales with the University Glee Club of New York City, of which I was a member, I had the great privilege to present these two volumes to the Bodleian Library. We were then invited to sing in the magnificent convocation room whose "ceiling was carved two years before your man Mr. Columbus put his foot upon your continent," as Mr. Vaisey expressed it to us.

Another remarkable acquisition through which my life was enriched and ultimately changed was the purchase of a 150-page scrapbook from Swann's Auction in New York. The scrapbook was a compilation of photos, letters, prints, drawings, coats of arms, etc., by a Mr. Ridgell Trout, who spent some forty years compiling data to prove that Edward de Vere, the seventeenth Earl of Oxford, was the true author of all the works attributed to William Shakespeare. I became intrigued with this proposition and subsequently spent years doing my own research. I now firmly believe that Edward de Vere is the true writer and join with hundreds of scholars in this view.

In the past twenty years I have used my library as an aid in teaching the history of illuminated manuscripts, early printed books, great libraries of the world, etc. Collecting books has been an exhilarating adventure. It is my hope that in the present generation of students at Rutgers many will share this quest.

Works Cited

Amadís De Gaul; a Poem in Three Books. 1803. Freely translated from the first part of the French version of Nicolas de Heberay... with notes, by William Stewart Rose. London: T. Cadell.

Amadís of Gaul Books I and II: A Novel of Chivalry of the 14th Century Presumably First Written in Spanish: Revised and Reworded by Garci Rodrígues de Montalvo prior to 1505, translated from the putative princeps of Saragossa, 1508. 1974. Lexington, KY: The UP of Kentucky.

Barker, Nicholas. 1985. *Aldus Manutius and the Development of Greek Script & Type in the Fifteenth Century.* Sandy Hook, CT: Chiswick Book Shop.

Barolini, Helen. 1991. *Aldus and His Dream Book.* Ithaca, NY: Italica Press.

Buzás, Ladislaus. 1986. *German Library History, 800–1945.* Trans. William D. Boyd. Jefferson, NC: McFarland.

Davis, Martin. 1995. *Aldus Manutius: Printer and Publisher of Renaissance Venice.* Malibu, CA: J. Paul Getty Museum.

Douen, Orentin. 1967. *Clément Marot et le Psautier Huguenot.* Amsterdam: Schippers.

Gardy, Frederic Louis. 1960. *Bibliographie des oeuvres, théologiques, littéraires, historiques et juridiques de Théodore de Bèze.* Geneva: E. Droz.

Garin, Eugenio. 1952. *Prosatori latini del Quattrocento.* Milan: R. Ricciardi.

Haebler, Konrad. 1967. *[Handbuch der Inkunabelkunde. English.] The Study of Incunabula.* New York: Kraus Reprint.

Hellinga, Wytze Gs. and Lotte. 1966. *The Fifteenth-century Printing Types of the Low Countries.* Trans. D.A.S. Reid. Amsterdam: Hertzberger.

Hind, Arthur Mayger. 1935. *An Introduction To A History of Woodcut, With a Detailed Survey of Work Done in the Fifteenth Century.* New York: Constable.

Hindman, Sandra. ed. 1982. *The Early Illustrated Book: Essays in Honor of Lessing J. Rosenwald.* Washington, DC: Library of Congress.

Johns, Francis. 1988. Notes on Two Unreported Editions of Clement Marot by Denys De Harsy, 1534. *Bibliotheque d'Humainisme et Renaissance* 1: 87–93.

Johnson, A.F. 1938. The Sixteenth Century. In *A History of The Printed Book,* ed. Lawrence C. Wroth, 121–156. New York: The Limited Editions Club.

Joseph, George. 1985. *Clément Marot.* Boston: Twayne.

Kristeller, Paul Oskar. 1966. *Eight Philosophers of the Italian Renaissance.* Stanford, CA: Stanford UP.

Landau, David. 1994. *The Renaissance Print, 1470–1550.* New Haven: Yale UP.

Leach, Eleanor W. 1982. Illustration as Interpretation in Brant's and Dryden's Edition of Vergil. In *The Early Illustrated Book: Essays in Honor of Lessing J. Rosenwald.* Washington, ed. Sandra Hindman, 175–210. DC: Library of Congress.

Levarie, Norma. 1994. *The Art & History of Books.* New Castle, DE: Oak Knoll Press and The British Library.

Lowry, Martin. 1979. *The World of Aldus Manutius*. Ithaca, NY: Cornell UP.

Lowry, Martin. 1991. *Nicholas Jenson and the Rise of Venetian Publishing in Renaissance Europe*. Oxford: Basil Blackwell.

Madden, D.H. 1924. *A Chapter of Mediaeval History*. London: J. Murray.

Mongan, Elizabeth. ed. 1940. *The First Printers and Their Books*, compiled by Elizabeth Mongan and Edwin Wolf II. Philadelphia, PA: Free Library.

Morison, Stanley. 1960. *Four Centuries of Fine Printing*. New Edition [i.e. 4th rev. (reset) ed.). New York: Barnes & Noble Inc.

Morison, Stanley. 1997. *Letter Forms, Typographic and Scriptorial*. Point Roberts, WA: Hartley & Marks Publishers.

Oswald, John Clyde. 1928. *A History of Printing: Its Development Through Five Hundred Years*. NY: Appleton.

Pollard, Alfred W. 1901. Book Illustration in the Fifteenth Century. *The Library* II:194–209.

Pollard, Alfred W. 1926. *Early Illustrated Books*. 3rd ed. London: Kegan Paul.

Proctor, Robert. 1900. *The Printing of Greek in The Fifteenth Century*. Oxford: Oxford UP.

Roylance, Dale. 1986. *European Graphic Arts: The Art of the Book from Gutenberg to Picasso*. Princeton, NJ: Princeton University Library.

Rath, Erich von. 1938. The Spread of Printing in the Fifteenth Century. In *A History of The Printed Book*, ed. Lawrence C. Wroth, 59–120. New York: Limited Editions Club.

Rytz, Walther. 1936. *Pflanzenaquarelle des Hans Weiditz aus dem Jahre 1529*. Bern: Haupt.

Sacchetti, Franco. 1970. *Novelle*. Milano: Fabbri.

Stannard, Jerry. 1969. The Herbal as a Medical Document. In *Bulletin of the History of Medicine* 43: 212–220.

Steinberg, S.H. 1961. *Five Hundred Years of Printing*. Harmondsworth: Penguin.

Stillwell, Margaret Bingham. 1972. *The Beginning of The World of Books, 1450–1470*. New York: Bibliographical Society of America.

Thomas, Henry. 1916. *The Romance of Amadis of Gaul*. 2d ed. Porto: Typographia da Emprêsa Litteraria e Typographica.

Timperley, C.H. 1839. *Dictionary of Printers and Printing*. London: H. Johnson.

Tory, Geoffroy. 1927. *Champ fleury*. Trans. George B. Ives. New York: Grolier Club.

Ullman, Berthold L., and Stadter, Philip. 1972. *The Public Library of Renaissance Florence*. Padova: Antenore.

Key to Abbreviations

Adams	Adams, Herbert Mayow. 1967. *Catalogue of Books Printed on the Continent of Europe, 1501–1600, in Cambridge Libraries.* London: Cambridge University Press.
Baudrier	Baudrier, Henri Louis. 1895–1921. *Bibliographie Lyonnaise.* Lyon: Librairie ancienne d'Auguste Brun.
BN	Paris. *Bibliothèque nationale.* Départment des imprimés. 1897–. *Catalogue généél des livres imprimés de la Bibliothèque nationale.* Paris: Impr. Nationale.
Duff	Duff, Edward Gordon. 1978. *Fifteenth Century English Books: A Bibliography of Books and Documents Printed in England and of Books for the English Market Printed Abroad.* Philadelphia: R. West.
Éditions parisiennes	Moreau, Briggite. *Inventive chronologique des Éditions parisiennes du XVI siècle.* Paris: Impr. municipale, 1972–.
Goff	Goff, Frederick R. 1964 *Incunabula in American Libraries.* New York: Bibliographical Society of America.
Goff (Suppl.)	Goff, Frederick R. 1972. *Incunabula… A Supplement.* New York: Bibliographical Society of America.
GW	*Gesamtkatalog der Wiegendrucke.* 1925–. Leipzig: K. W. Hiersemann.
Renouard	Renouard, A. A. 1803. *Annals de l'imprimerie des Alde.* Paris: A. A. Renouard.
STC	Pollard, Alfred William, and Redgrave, G. R. 1929. *A Short-Title Catalogue of Books Printed in England, Scotland & Ireland and of English Books Printed Aboard, 1475–1640.* London: Bibliographical Society.
VD16	*Verzeichnis der im deutschen Sprachbereich erschienen Drucke des XVI. Jahrunderts* (ed. Irmgard Bezzel). 1983–1997. Stuttgart: A. Hiersemann.